How To Build Your
Dream Garage

How To Build Your
Dream Garage

Lee Klancher

motorbooks

For Uncle Pat, my family's professional builder

First published in 2008 by Motorbooks, an imprint of MBI Publishing Company, 400 First Avenue North, Suite 300, Minneapolis, MN 55401 USA

Motorbooks titles are also available at discounts in bulk quantity for industrial or sales-promotional use. For details write to Special Sales Manager at MBI Publishing Company, 400 First Avenue North, Suite 300, Minneapolis, MN 55401 USA.

To find out more about our books, join us online at www.motorbooks.com.

Library of Congress Cataloging-in-Publication Data

Klancher, Lee, 1966-
  How to build your dream garage / Lee Klancher.
    p. cm.
  ISBN 978-0-7603-3173-6 (sb)
  1. Garages. 2. Workshops. I. Title.
TL153.K585 2008
690'.898—dc22

                    2007049745

Editor: Dennis Pernu
Designer: Chris Fayers

Printed in Singapore

Front cover: Bill Cotter's garage in the Seattle area is an old warehouse filled with a collection of vintage race cars, a flathead-powered Ford roadster, and other collector cars. The walls are covered with everything from go-karts to F1 race suits. Cotter (right) chats with DeWitt Whitman while Roger Kennedy wrenches.

Frontispiece: Air tools make wrenching a bit simpler, and nearly every power tool under the sun is available, from impact wrenches and ratchets to cut-off tools and sanders.

Title page: This garage is a cleverly outfitted warehouse. Note that the workbench is tucked underneath the loft.

Back cover: The metal walls line the well-designed workspace in a motorcycle customization shop. Metal walls are an economical way to give a space a flashy, industrial look.

Opposite: Your dream garage doesn't have to be huge or expensive. This heated and insulated space is outfitted so that owner Gary Snell can squeeze in a full-sized Oliver farm tractor for restoration. When he's not mired in a restoration project, his John Deere lawn tractor is stored inside the space.

About the author
Lee Klancher has been publishing his words and photographs since 1992. He has authored six illustrated books, photographed a half-dozen calendars, and written for dozens of magazines, including *Minneapolis-St. Paul*, *Motorcycle Escape*, and *Robb Report Motorcycling*. His work as a traveling journalist has taken him to the Bolivian Amazon on an off-road ride with South American dignitaries, and to Hope, Alaska, to interview former truck drivers in dive bars. In 2004, he built a 1,000-square-foot heated garage/office that's larger than his St. Paul, Minnesota, home.

CONTENTS

ACKNOWLEDGMENTS

Thanks to the people who helped make this book happen. To my research assistant, Kathy Pilney, thanks for putting in the long hours. This book would not have happened without your dedication and smart use of resources. To the Motorbooks crew, thanks to all for making this book come together, particularly to editor Dennis Pernu for all his diligence and hard work throughout the process, and to Zack Miller, for his support of my freelance endeavor (if I had a real job, I wouldn't have had time to create this book!).

Thanks are also due to the garage lovers who showed me their places: Gordon Apker, John Coffee, Bill Cotter, Jack Dant, Hector Garcia and the boys at the Texican Chop Shop, John Goodman, Roger Kennedy, Kevin Manley, Ken McBride, Bill Nichols, Mark Triebold of Crossroads Performance, DeWitt Whitman, and Sam Wheeler Sr.

I also want to thank the people who helped find photos, referred me to others, and provided materials and information: Brad Barquist at Onrax; Brian and Kari Cornell; Tom Cotter; Wendy Danks from the Twin Cities Builder's Association; Gigi DiGiacomo at DiGiacomo Homes and Renovation; Len Faria at Shelter-Kit; Anil Gupta at Diamond Life; Paul Husnik at Husnik Homes; Patrick Illfrey at Citadel Floors; Gregg Irvin at Xceltronix; George Karonis at R. E. Williams; Mark Larson at Rehkamp Larson; Laurin Leih at SlideLok; Dennis McPherson; Sherry Moeller at *Washington Spaces* magazine; Laura Orfield from Orfield Design and Construction; Randy Nelson at SwissTrax; Jason Noble at Diamondlife; Pat Plautz at Valley Cabinets; and photographer Michael Stewart.

A big thanks and a couple of beers are due to the guys willing to help out on the how-to projects, Craig O'Connell and Kris Palmer.

Last, to John Koharski, who did what he does best and shook down all the right people to make this happen.

INTRODUCTION

The garage is one of the last bastions of hands-on activities in an automated, hands-off world. It's a place to indulge your hobbies, whether that means restoring a Norton Commando, tinkering with your Citroën 2CV, or tuning the fuel-injection unit in your big-block Chevy hot rod. Those hours in the garage are your chance to get away from the daily grind. Maybe smash a finger or two.

Your garage is your sanctuary. The politics in your garage are simple. Do I need a 3/8- or 7/16-inch wrench? Will that exhaust pipe come off if enough heat and pressure is applied? Am I out of beer?

In the complex world that surrounds us, these simple pleasures are a joy.

Building your dream garage should also be a joy. I can tell you from experience that it most definitely is, but there are pitfalls. I built mine in 2004 to house my office and small collection of off-road and adventure motorcycles, and I found myself wishing for this book. I discovered some good resources that helped, but there wasn't a book that walked me through the process.

And I'm a book guy. Since I was knee-high, I've been happy with nothing more than a comfortable chair and a good book. As much as I dig my motorcycle habit, my book habit is stronger.

So it was only natural that I looked for the right book to help me build my garage. And when I couldn't find it, I decided to write it.

This book is designed for people who are into some kind of hobby that takes place in the garage. And I assumed that you, like me, don't like to waste money paying someone to do something you can do yourself. So I included a number of simple step-by-step projects that pretty much anyone can do at home, adding some sweat equity to your garage. This book is for you, my friend. My hope is you won't make the mistakes I did.

You see, as an old friend of mine likes to say, I have gone ahead and made most of the stupid mistakes so you don't have to. The territory I've explored is a landscape littered with things that didn't work out so well, from a heating system that didn't quite match my needs until it was redone (twice) to a design that went through more revisions than the story of James Dean's fatal crash.

Yes, I'm great at stupid mistakes. Might be my strongest talent.

But my mistakes are your benefit—I can pass my hard-earned knowledge to you in the pages of this book. Not only can I tell you how to avoid the mistakes I made, I can also clue you in on how to make your garage cool and save money at the same time. Let's face it: the world is an expensive place, and as much as I enjoy motorcycling, I'm not willing to spend every spare nickel on it. In fact, I take great pride in the things I can build, swap, or pick up on Craigslist or eBay for dirt cheap.

I came by that honestly, as my dad was the king of all cheapskates. He and my mother raised three kids on two teachers' salaries. We grew up with decent clothes (that Mom made), good food (thanks to the garden), and even a new garage (my uncle and his long-haired construction crew came over and built it for Dad in a weekend in exchange for all the beer they could drink).

We used to call Dad "Scrooge" because we didn't get what he was doing back then. I appreciate it now and have inherited some of those tendencies. There's a running gag in this book about that, and you'll find lots of references to "Mr. Cheapskate." I'm talking about being able to get things done right for next to nothing using guerilla tactics such as shopping at re-use centers, buying rejected stock from cabinetmakers, and so on. That doesn't mean that the end result—your garage—will be a cheaply constructed dump. Quite the opposite. My mission was to build a great garage and not spend $60,000 doing so. I did it and learned a lot that can help you do even better.

So if you're a Mr. Cheapskate like me, I think you'll find this book helpful. Read on. I want to save you money.

I'm assuming, by the way, that you are like me and interested in reading about how things work, even if you don't do the work yourself. Things like how to calculate electrical circuit needs are probably not something you are going to do at home, but I explain the concept so that you can at least understand what the electrician is telling you.

When it comes to things you will do yourself, such as coat your garage floor, I've given you the basic steps and quizzed the pros doing the work to provide you with the tricks and techniques that you won't find in the directions on the bucket. Or I did it myself, screwed it up, and have passed on the knowledge to you!

I hope you enjoy some time in the armchair as well as out working in the garage and that your wrench-and-beer palace becomes your sanctuary. Just don't let the neighbor wander in and talk politics.

How to Use This Book

Throughout, you'll find icons that call out areas of particular interest and make this book faster and easier to use.

Cheapskate Special—Save big money with the points these icons mark.

Garage Geek Alert—If you are into detail, watch for this icon, which indicates places your anal-retentive nature will be rewarded.

Smart Money—Indicates cases in which even cheapskates are better off ponying up the dough.

High-Tech Garage Goodies—Marks the inclusion of cool technology for your garage.

CHAPTER 1
THE STRUCTURE

If you already have a garage built, you can skip this chapter. But if you are building a new structure, this chapter is where you want to start.

If you are starting from scratch and building a new garage, you are faced with a lot of options. Think them through carefully before proceeding!

There are four basic considerations to keep in mind when building a new garage: your available space, the zoning restrictions in your city or township, your budget, and your needs.

AVAILABLE SPACE

Those who own significant acreage are the lucky ones. They have plenty of space to build a giant 50x200 space with shops, bays, and indoor tracks. For the rest of the world, how much space you have available will determine what you build.

In today's world, the bulk of the population lives on a city lot of some kind, either urban or suburban. In your case, your options are going to be much more limited.

One of the things you are going to need in order to lay out your garage plan is a plot plan. This is a drawing that shows the locations of everything on your property. You can have a surveying company do one of these for you. This is useful to have if you sell the home, and you will most likely need one when you apply for your building permit, so getting one early in the process is not a bad idea.

If you want to have a rough idea of the lot before you pay for a plot plan, you can draw one yourself. Buy a pad of graph paper and enlist someone to help you measure out the lot carefully. Draw in the location of the house, the property lines, and the locations of any big stuff (sheds, trees, etc.). Then, make a photocopy of your drawing. In fact, make lots of photocopies, and put the original someplace safe.

 Now, start drawing. See what fits where and how you might best use the space you have available. Don't be afraid to show your sketches to friends and family (who have an interest), and ask for helpful suggestions. Magazines are another great source for ideas—home-building magazines occasionally have garage specials that feature lots of interesting spaces. You can also pick up a number of books that showcase stunning garages around the United States and Canada.

Manny Barbosa's garage is stunningly finished inside, a place to spend time with your vehicles rather than a working space where you change oil and rebuild carburetors. Washingtonspaces.com

Whatever you have to work with as your garage's structure, the finishing choices you make will play a big role in how it comes out. Manny Barbosa's Ferrari and Ducati palace is proof that attached garages don't have to be boring. Washingtonspaces.com

Remember that you will need a driveway and will be driving near and around the garage. My neighbor suggested I move my garage 5 feet farther back than my original drawing indicated so I could turn my car around in my driveway and pull out (rather than back out) into my fairly busy street. I mentally thank him nearly every time I leave the driveway.

Also, bear in mind any outdoor spaces such as patios and play areas that you want to incorporate into your plan.

LOCAL BUILDING REGULATIONS

After you determine the space you have available, you need to know what you can do with the space. Your city hall or other local government agency creates building codes, which are very specific guidelines that determine what you can and cannot build. Building codes have gotten increasingly complex over the years, and you will want to become familiar with these in order to make your plan.

You can find out the city regulations online, or stop by the city hall and get a copy of the latest guidelines. You'll need to know if there are restrictions on the size of your garage, including the square footage and roof height. You'll also want to check out the setbacks, which dictate how close to the property line you can build.

You will most likely need a building permit. Permit applications usually require you to submit a plan (this varies by municipality from a simple drawing to a complete architectural plan) and pay a fee (though fees vary wildly, expect to pay several hundred dollars).

I found it easiest to just talk with someone to learn what's permitted. Your municipality's building inspector is a possible source for this information, but bear in mind that this person will not tell you any of the "tricks" you can use.

Another good source for this kind of information is your contractor, if you use one. They generally know most of the local regulations, as well as tricks of the trade. They also may know the local inspectors personally and will ideally have a positive relationship with them.

Long-time residents can also be good sources for information about codes, inspectors, and the art of dealing with your local government. I happened to have a neighbor who was a former construction engineer in town, and he provided a lot of useful information about what you can and can't do in my town.

If you find you want to do something that is in violation of a city regulation, you can generally make your case to the city council (or the planning council, depending on the size of your community) and apply for a variance, which is basically written permission to violate a city regulation. This process typically takes anywhere from two to six months, however, and may require you to get written permission from your neighbors.

Once you are familiar with the local building codes, you can go back to your drawing and check that all the setbacks, heights, and so on are correct.

BUDGET

How much can you afford? That's always a question with garages and one you want to pay careful attention to. The garage isn't going to add a ton of value to a home. Yes, having a place to keep cars out of the rain is a plus, but to most people that heated, marble-floored four-car palace with an in-floor lift and built-in welding plugs is not worth more than a simple two-car, cement-floor structure.

Plus, there's the matter of marital harmony to consider. The reality of the matter is if you end up spending $120,000 to add a garage that adds $20,000 of value to

Kevin Manley's 17-car garage shows off how your landscape can be used to create a lot of interior space without the exterior looking out of balance. The house is built on a lake lot, with a bank descending to the water on the back side. The ground-level garage is a double-deep, double-wide space used to park daily drivers and store lawn equipment. Living space and a rear deck were built above the garage. A drive runs to the left of the garage and down to a lower level on the lake side. Two lower garage doors on the back side open to a nicely finished garage that houses Manley's collector cars.

If you are designing your garage from scratch, you can dress up the front of the building with a porch or patio. The door that owner Gordon Apker is closing leads to about 40,000 square feet of garage space, all cleverly tucked into a hill and hidden behind old outbuildings and this gazebo.

your home, your marriage is probably going to suffer. If you are like most of us, spending $120K on a place to change the oil is going to raise hell.

So there are lots of reasons to do a good budget.

If you have enough cash to cover the cost of building a garage, you are golden. A simple two-car garage can be put up for $20,000 or so by a contractor in most parts of the United States. Material costs on such a project range from $5,000 for a kit to about $15,000 for fancier buildings. Obviously, the more elaborate your garage, the more costs rise.

If you are borrowing money, your bank can help out. The most typical arrangement is to take out a second mortgage on your house. This only applies to people who have enough equity to borrow against. Your banker can help you get a home-value estimate to see how much equity you have. An estimator can give you an idea of how much completing the garage will increase your home value.

I'm a spreadsheet nut and found a budget tremendously useful when I did my garage. As with most people who build, I underestimated what I would spend, but at least I was in the ballpark and didn't end up spending more on the garage than my property is worth.

 If you are a cheapskate, one way you can save significant amounts of money is by doing some of the finish work yourself. In addition to helping you save money, this route will give you the satisfaction of doing that work yourself.

Before you decide to tackle any work yourself, you need to assess your skills. Unless you are a finish carpenter, you will pay some kind of price in terms of the quality of the finish. If, for example, you have never hung sheetrock and have no friends who can help, your sheetrock will probably look a little rough around the edges. If you don't care, go to it. Just be aware of the drawbacks going into the job.

You can avoid a lot of do-it-yourself (DIY) mistakes by picking up a couple of home improvement books that tell you how to hang sheetrock, build walls, wire the building, and so on. Reading books is no substitute for hiring a pro, but it will help you avoid the most basic mistakes.

If you have friends who are experienced with this kind of work and are willing to help, even for a few hours, you have a huge edge. Be sure they can do the work well, though! Help from people who do the job poorly is not really help at all.

The Apker garage is a sprawling warehouse that was built about 50 yards back from this old barn. Hip roofs are good choices when you are planning to use the space above the first level. The design maximizes the room in the second floor. The look has to fit with your place, however. When you build a garage, consider not only the design of your home but the type of structures throughout the neighborhood.

Also, consider hiring a professional just to help out for a couple of hours. This is way cheaper than paying for the entire job and means that you will learn how to do it right. This may apply if you are doing the wiring yourself, for example. Hire a pro for an hour up front to discuss the job, and another hour or two on the back end to go over what you did and point out mistakes. You will still make mistakes, but will avoid the really stupid, expensive kinds of mistakes.

See the sample budget sidebar to determine how to calculate how much doing the work yourself will save. This can help you make smart decisions about what to do at home and what to have contracted out.

Remember that unless you want to learn how to do the work or will enjoy it, you are probably better off just paying the money and having a professional do the job. Projects that you do at home are tremendously satisfying, but they also will require some long hours of work that can be tedious and grueling.

If you can build the entire garage yourself, budgeting is much more complex because you'll need to figure out material costs. Places like your local lumber yard or even a "big-box" home chain can help. You can also find online calculators that allow you to get ballpark costs for DIY projects.

Building your own garage is not out of the question, particularly if you can get help from someone who has done this kind of work before. The smartest example of this I have seen is Jack Dant, who paid a highly regarded architecture firm, Rehkamp Larson Architects, to draw up his floor plan and then worked with a friend who was a structural engineer to create the detailed drawing he needed to build the structure. He paid to have the concrete floor poured and did the rest of the work himself. The project took him three years to finish, but the end result was a beautifully finished painting studio above a simple garage and workshop.

But before you can determine material costs, you need to decide the size and design of your garage (see later sections for more information on this), then create a specifi-

The garage is a great place to hang out, and this portion of the Apker garage is a reminder to plan for recreational space in your structure.

Above: *When laying out rooms, consider using several garage doors to provide access. Even in a small garage, this can make it simpler to access your equipment. A small overhead door in the back of a residential garage, for example, can make it easy to get out your mower, motorcycles, ATVs, or other small vehicles.*

Right: *The Apker place is referred to as the "Chicken Coop," an ironic reference to the modest exterior that conceals a huge car and memorabilia collection.*

cation sheet. If you want an idea of the level of detail you'll need to get a bid, check out the specs that appear with the sample budget sidebar. If you work with a contractor, they can help you develop this.

Once you have your project spec'd, you can get bids and create a budget for the entire project. Note that it's also helpful to make a list of all the goodies you want to add to the garage so you have a pretty good idea of how much money this project will require.

continued on page 26

Sample Project Budget

Here's a sample budget. The "Estimate" column represents what it will cost you to have the work done by a contractor (materials and labor), the "DIY Cost" column represents how much you will pay for the materials necessary to do the job, and the "DIY Savings" is the amount of money you will save by doing the work yourself.

These numbers come from actual bids done in 2007. If you want to create a similar sheet for yourself, I recommend you get formal bids or at least make a phone call to your local supplier to get a rough idea of what materials will cost. These costs fluctuate tremendously, and labor costs vary depending on where you live.

On the 24x28 structure below, these numbers indicate you can save nearly $20,000 by doing some of the work yourself. And note that the work I included—building walls, coating a floor, hanging sheetrock, and so on—are all tasks that nearly anyone with the time and inclination is more than capable of doing.

The last column represents how many dollars per hour you save by doing this work. If you are taking home $213 per hour, well, don't bother doing any of this unless you really enjoy it. Otherwise, you might want to at least consider doing some of the work yourself.

Note that the dollars-per-hour calculation is also a good way to see what is worth doing yourself and what you are better off paying to have done. I saved a significant amount of money on my garage's patio, for example, but it required several weekends of grueling work and, finally, calling in favors from everyone I knew in order to assemble a large enough crew to finish it.

Keep in mind that some of these DIY projects require help from a neighbor, friend, or relative. Hanging sheetrock, for example, is something that pros can do solo, but mere mortals should attempt it only with a partner.

I created this sheet in Excel, as it allows you to include formulas that calculate dollars per hour, totals, etc. Even if you are not into the DIY scene, something like this simple budget calculator can give you a realistic picture of what your project will cost.

Finally, you can add all the goodies (lifts, welders, and so on) you are going to include in the garage. Just don't leave *that* list lying around where your spouse can see it.

As I mentioned, the prices in this bid are based on 2007 rates in the Midwest. The bid was spec'd for a modest-sized structure with in-floor heating tubing installed.

The specs on the bid are 24x28 garage; 9-foot 2x6 stud walls; green-treated sill plate; two steel insulated service doors; one 18x8-foot overhead garage door with opener and two remotes; one keyless entry; four double-hung windows; 10–12 roof pitch with room and attic truss; 2-foot on-center (OC) 1/2-inch oriented strand board (OSB) sheathing; 7/16-inch wall sheathing; 4-inch vinyl siding; 2-foot aluminum soffit and fascia; 4-inch concrete floor with 8x12-inch footing; 1 1/2-inch 4x8-foot Styrofoam sheeting under concrete with 1/2-inch PEX tubing; bolt anchors as per print, as city code; $800 electrical allowance; floor drain to be stubbed to outside of building; does not include inside finish work.

Item	Estimate	DIY Cost	DIY Hours	DIY Savings	Dollars/ Hour
24x28 Building (as spec'd)	$28,000				
Additions					
20x12 Asphalt Drive	$3,000				
30x25 Patio and 4x25 Walkway	$8,400	$2,500	84	$5,900	$70
Water Shark On-Demand Electric Water Heater	$400				
Electrician to Hook up Water Heater and Wire Garage	$400				
Permit Fees	$250				
24x28 Floor for Upstairs (1/2-inch plywood)	$2,000	$350	25	$1,650	$66
Installing Stairway	$500	$75	2	$425	$213
Coating 24x28 Floor	$2,000	$500	6	$1,500	$250
12x2 Workbench	$1,000	$250	8	$750	$94
24-foot Shop Dividing Wall	$1,500	$250	8	$1,250	$156
Sheetrocking Garage	$2,500	$446	30	$2,054	$68
Taping and Mudding Sheetrock	$800	$100	20	$700	$35
Insulating Structure	$2,000	$289	40	$1,711	$43
Lighting (Interior and Exterior)	$1,500	$400	8	$1,100	$138
Security System	$3,000	$500	6	$2,500	$417
Total	$57,250		237	$19,540	$82
Cost with DIY Savings	$37,710				

When you're designing a new garage, by far the simplest route is a separate structure. You avoid the fire codes associated with garages that are attached to living spaces, and you'll add an entirely new building to your property. Note that this one uses a second floor and small dormers to add space. A second floor is an economical way to add space to your structure. Washingtonspaces.com

Above: *A small space can still be a garage palace with the right finishing touches, such as this checkerboard-patterned floor tile.* SwissTrax

Right: *When building from scratch, consider adding living and recreational spaces to your design. This stunning garage uses a roof-top patio and additional room and entry to transcend mere garagedom. You'll need the help of an architect to create a design like this, but working with a good architect is a small relative cost.* Vujovich Designs

When building in an urban space, one major consideration is your city's building codes. You will likely face restrictions regarding your garage's square footage, roof height, and distances from the lot line and your house. In some cases, a small, efficient structure is your best choice. Vujovich Designs

continued from page 19

NEEDS

What kind of space needs do you have? Well, to start with, what are you going to put in the garage? Make a list of the big items, and you'll have an idea.

Bear in mind that three-car garages are of value these days. More and more regular people are interested in room to park two cars and store a boat, bicycles, lawn mower, or the other typical home goodies.

I'm assuming you bought this book because you are a car or motorcycle nut of some kind, and that means you probably lust after space for four, five, or more cars. That's the kind of space that won't add value unless the buyer is also an enthusiast, so be careful. Make sure you can afford it, and don't expect to get much return on the investment if you sell your home.

But don't hesitate to add a three-car space. That's something most home purchasers these days will appreciate.

Also, a few suggestions. If your space allows it, consider going extra deep with the garage. The standard depth of a typical garage is 24 feet. That's fine if all you want to do is park in the garage.

Adding another 6 or 10 feet of depth will not break the bank, and it will allow you space to build a nice workbench area, store anything from motorcycles to welding equipment, or comfortably park that 21-foot-long Cadillac Fleetwood or Ford F-350 Super Duty Crew Cab you've been dreaming about.

Another increasingly popular addition is a carport on the side. These are common in southern climates. In the north, they are useful for keeping the snow off a boat or

When you have an elevated lot, you have a wonderful opportunity to design an extraordinary garage. This one puts an extra-deep, two-car space down below and an art studio up above. Note how nicely owner Jack Dant matched the design of the house, right down to the Craftsman details.

A log building is an option worth considering for a garage, particularly if you are handy and ambitious. You can buy build-it-yourself log structures for fairly reasonable prices, and the end result will be energy efficient and unique. SwissTrax

extra car during the winter. Consider working one into your plan if you have lots of vehicles and some of them don't have to be kept in the garage.

 If you are into planning, get out your graph paper and draw a space that is approximately the size you need. Bear in mind that width will be determined by materials. If you are using prefabricated roof trusses, they come in standard widths ranging from 16 to 40 feet. Note that the depth of the garage should be divisible by 4 feet.

So draw a couple of different sizes of your garage on the graph paper.

Next, measure all of the things you are going to put in the garage (cars, motorcycles, trucks, snowblowers, benches, etc.). Either draw them on the graph paper or cut out small pieces of graph paper in the same size and label them.

Using these cutouts, you can see how things fit in the garage and try out different layouts. You can purchase a kit to do this from a company called Design Works, Inc. The kit comes with graph paper and several sheets of clear plastic draw-to-scale outlines of chairs, tables, and appliances (you have to cut out your own cars and motorcycles).

Note that if you do this, you are a certifiable garage nut, or just plain nuts. I spent hours doing this—I believe I fit into both categories.

CHOOSING A DESIGN

This can be the trickiest portion of building a new garage. The best way to get ideas for your design is to do some research. First of all, browse some of the many plan vendors on the Internet. Some have photo galleries that show interesting designs.

Books and magazines are also a decent way to help you choose your design, as are paying attention as you drive to and from work and asking friends and family if they know of any really interesting garages.

Also, consider the style of your house and your neighborhood. You will want to match the roof's pitch and/or height to that of your house if you want the two to be complementary. And you (and your neighbors) don't want your garage to be wildly out of place. A nicely done Craftsman-style garage in an older urban neighborhood of similarly styled homes might add a bit of class, for example, while a two-story steel-sided monstrosity will look out of place and awkward.

Detached structures are the easiest and most economical to build. Adding an attached garage is a hassle—you'll have to install a fireproof barrier between the garage and your living space, and if you live in a cooler climate, you'll need footings to keep the garage from frost-heaving and separating from your house.

continued on page 32

Right: *Another option for your dream garage is to renovate an existing structure. This old shed serves as a home for owner Kim Spaulding's collection of antique farm tractors.*

Opposite: *Steel buildings can be great solutions, depending on your needs. They are cheap to put up and great for covering large spaces. This shop in San Angelo, Texas, is co-owned by members of the band Los Lonely Boys and custom car wizard Hector Garcia (far right). The building was purchased because band member Henry Garza worked in a shop housed in this building while growing up. The Texican Chop Shop's building isn't fancy, but their custom creations are over the top.*

Below: *When you need a lot of space for machinery, a steel outbuilding is a great choice. You can have an uninsulated 30x50-foot steel shed built for about $20,000. If you are willing to construct the building, you can find build-it-yourself kits that cost less than $10,000 for a 30x40-foot building.*

Apply for Permits and Variances

What You'll Need:

Permit and/or variance forms (from city hall)

Patience

Knowledge of your area's building codes

Time: 1–6 months

Tab: $200+

Permits

Any time you improve your home with any kind of electrical, mechanical, or construction process, you probably need to pull a permit. Building garages, adding security systems, and increasing the number of outlets are all processes that typically require a permit.

If you hire a contractor, they should be responsible for applying for the permits. Make sure this is specified in your contract.

Pulling the proper permits will help your resale value and provide some peace of mind knowing that the additions are safely executed. That isn't to say the process will be a pleasure. City officials are like anyone else—some of them are great to work with, others not so much. The keys are to budget enough time, do the work right, and know what's permitted and what's not.

Your starting point is to find out what's required. Good resources are generally available online through your city's Web site. Some areas have tremendous resources for this.

In general, some of the issues facing homeowners building garages include the setback (how far from the property line and your own home you can build), height restrictions, total square-foot restrictions, and time limits on how long it will take you to build the structure.

Start by doing your reading. Check out the local city hall or county seat Web site. Most areas have building codes and permits available online. If you have questions, see if you can make an appointment with your city inspector and go over your concerns.

If you do spend some time face to face with the inspector, be polite. This person can make your life living hell—try to remember that before you launch into your copyrighted rant about how government has

insinuated itself into every aspect of your life and you're thinking of moving to Bolivia. Save that for your buddies and stick to the facts.

Variances

If your building plans include some aspects that violate city code, you are going to need a variance. Bear in mind that you probably can't get a variance to, say, build a commercial puppy farm on a property that is zoned residential. You probably can get a variance if you need to violate a setback restriction by 2 feet because you have an oddly shaped lot. In general, variances are supposed to allow people to develop their property as their neighbors do.

If you need a variance, you will most likely also need time. You'll need a detailed plan for the improvements you'd like to do, plot plans that show your property and the location of the new addition, architectural drawings for any construction changes, and your local government's application forms. You'll also probably have to write a check, and you may have to acquire the consent of your neighbors within a set distance (100 feet of the lot line is typical in urban areas). This means canvassing the neighborhood and explaining what you plan to do and convincing people to sign the form for you.

Once all that's done, your variance is by no means guaranteed. If everyone on your block agrees with your proposal and signs yes on the variance form and your change is fairly standard, you may be able to simply take it down to city hall and get the signature of the building inspector.

More radical departures from city code require that the proposal be put in front of the city council. You may have to attend this meeting, explain your position, and wait for a vote to decide your fate. And if you have neighbors who object to your proposal, you may have to go through a public hearing about the issue. Any time you are dealing with meetings or hearings, you can expect the process to take a few months, at minimum, and it could easily drag out for six to eight months.

CITY OF OAKDALE

1584 HADLEY AV N O OAKDALE O MN O 55128
Phone (651) 739-5150 O Fax (651) 730-2820
www.ci.oakdale.mn.us

Building Permit Application

Job Address: _____

Description of work to be done: _____

Estimated Value of all work (including labor and material): $_____

Applicant: _____

        Day Phone (_____)_____   **Cell Phone** (_____)_____

Address: _____

City _____ **State** _____ **Zip** _____

Check One: S Property Owner   S Contractor (complete next line)

        License # _____ License Type_____ Exp. Date _____

Applicant Signature: _____ **Date:** _____

Issuance of a permit and inspections conducted do not constitute a guarantee of warranty from the City. The applicant hereby agrees to do all work in accordance with the ordinances of the City of Oakdale, State Building Code, and the requirements of the Building Department.

FOR CITY USE ONLY:

Permit Fee		Water Meter	
Plan Check		SAC	
Surcharge		City SAC	
Fire Surcharge		WAC	
Street Clean-up		Park Dedication	
SWMF		**PERMIT TOTAL**	$
Escrow Deposit (Pay by separate check)			$
		TOTAL FEES DUE	$

*Escrow will be refunded only to the entity depositing the funds.

Approvals: Bldg Dept. _____ _____ Eng. Dept. _____

Permit No. _____

Office Use Only:

Payment received in the form of: ____ Check (#   ) ____ Cash ____ Credit Card

Legal Description: _____

S:\Common\Building\BUILDING PERMIT APPLICATION.doc

Building permits are a standard part of building any new structure. The forms vary a bit in level of detail required, but most are similar to this one. City of Oakdale

continued from page 27
Finally, you can also design your own garage using software packages developed for the task. These are not always terribly simple to use, and you will need to consult with an architect or your contractor to make sure the garage you design is economical (and practical) to build.

Above and opposite: *Steel buildings are maintenance-free and fire-resistant, and most come with a 30-year warranty. If you want a heated shop, consider building a room inside the structure and insulating and heating that space.*

PLANS

Once you have settled on a design, you are going to need a formal plan (an architectural drawing). This very detailed drawing is the best way to get an accurate bid and is typically necessary to get a building permit as well. This needs to be more than just the plan you scratched out on graph paper, as all the specifications need to be included.

Predrawn garage plans are readily available and are adequate for simple garages without any custom features. You can find them in dozens of garage books, on the Internet, and at companies dedicated to garage plans. See the appendix for a list of sources for garage plans.

Plan perusing is great fun for the garage nut, and you'll find some interesting designs. Choose a few that you like. If you have a contractor, you can work together to select the final plan before you purchase it. Expect to pay between $20 and $75 for a good predrawn plan.

If you are building a garage that uses an unusual lot or custom features, have an architect draw up a plan for you. This is surprisingly affordable and one of the smartest places you can spend your money if you are building a custom-built garage. You can get a custom plan for as little as $200.

If the plan is well thought out and properly designed, odds are good that the resulting building will be what you want. With a lousy or poorly planned design, what do you think you'll get? For more information, see the sidebar on creating custom plans.

FINISHING THE STRUCTURE

Having a good plan for your garage doesn't mean you are done making decisions. You'll have to outfit the building properly. Here are some considerations you'll need to take into account as you work through the bid with your contractor.

Siding

Siding is the material that covers the outside of your structure, and your choices here will have the most dramatic effect on how the building looks—not to mention the property value. The simplest thing is to match what's on your house. But if you want to spice up your look, there are plenty of options to consider. One thought for you home improvement nuts is to side both your house and your new garage to give your entire place a new look.

The most durable way to side your building is in brick or stucco. Brick is incredibly durable and has some value as an insulating material as well. Stucco is a cement mixture that is put on top of chicken wire or a masonry product. The smooth, typically white or light-colored exterior look is common in Mission- and Spanish-style homes.

If you finish the structure in brick or stucco and add in vinyl or aluminum trim and fascia boards, you will have a maintenance-free structure that is incredibly durable and good-looking. The drawback here is cost—brick and stucco will cost at least double the price of wood or hardboard.

If you aren't doing brick or mortar, you will be siding the house with some kind of board. The most common types are horizontally mounted boards between 8 and 16 inches wide. These are typically installed as "lap" siding, which refers to the fact that the boards overlap.

Siding can also be mounted vertically, which works especially well on a high-peaked structure that is designed to look like a barn. Vertical siding typically has narrow slats over the joints.

Board siding is available in a variety of materials. Vinyl is cheap and lasts forever. You don't have to paint it, but vinyl will fade with time, and you'll have to replace it once it fades. If you go with vinyl siding, get it with insulation, and it will provide a durable, economical coat on your house.

Hardboard, or fiber cement, siding boards provide a good mix of relatively low cost, low maintenance, durability, and good looks. You can get it molded to look like cedar shakes or wood boards, and it can be painted or ordered precolored. It is more expensive than vinyl, but the return in longevity and look is well worth the extra dollars. Cheapskates, this is your choice for a good, durable coating.

Wood siding requires a lot of maintenance and, if you go with cedar, is also very expensive. The vertical "car-siding" used on barns and sheds is quite economical, but

continued on page 38

Create Custom Building Plans

THE STRUCTURE

What You'll Need: Local architect
Research
Planning
Time: 1–8 hours
Tab: $200–$1,200

When you have a garage in mind that departs from the ordinary or you are doing a remodel job, a custom plan is the best way to go. This tailors the space to your needs as well as your lot's physical properties.

You can, of course, try to draw the design yourself with a computer-aided design (CAD) program or on graph paper. While this is a good way to get your ideas on paper, creating your own plans without the help of a pro is risky business. You need someone who not only understands structural needs but also the local codes in order to create a complete design necessary for a well-built structure. The good news is that working with an architect on a custom plan may cost as little as $200 for a simple structure. More complex designs that incorporate two floors, hot tubs, and living space may cost you more, but $1,200 should cover most drawings.

Working with an architectural firm will give you not only a custom plan but the help of experienced professionals able to foresee issues and problems you might miss. You'll find an assortment of architectural firms that offer everything from a consultation to complete services that include design, planning, and contracting to have the work completed. See a list of resources and a few good firms in this book's appendix.

The first step is to determine what kind of structure you want and need. Put some time and thought into what is going to go into your garage, what kind of activities you'd like to do out there, and how you want the structure to look.

Your neighborhood can give you clues as to how your project should look. "You don't want the garage to look like it dropped in from heaven," says architect Laura Orfield. "A garage palace with columns is not going to look right in an old, modest neighborhood." Also, look at magazines, books, and Web sites for ideas on the look and features you'd like. Make a list of the things you find appealing, then prioritize and be prepared to let go of a few things if you need to meet your budget.

Bear in mind that you are going to want a site survey in order to do an architectural plan. A site survey is a precisely measured plot of your property that includes dimensions of everything on your lot. Nearly anyone who is doing remodeling should have one of these. It is also helpful if you ever plan to sell your house.

Once you know the structure you want, at least roughly, think about how much you want the architect to do. Do you want them to just draw up a plan? Or would you also like them to contract to have the work completed? (You can also call a couple of contractors yourself and talk informally about what you have in mind and see if they can give you ballpark ideas of the cost.)

One of the most important things to bring to your architect is a realistic budget. They need to know how much money you have to work with so they can plan accordingly. In order to get a good idea of what it might cost to do the work you have in mind, open your eyes to what's happening in the neighborhood around you. If someone has recently built a garage you like, stop in to ask for a tour. Most people love to show off their new projects and will be happy to show you around.

In order to find a good architect, start by asking people you know and trust. Put the word out and see what comes up. Also, you can go to the Yellow Pages or consult several Web sites such as the American Institute

A detailed plan is key to building your garage, and this hand-drawn example from Orfield Design shows all the detail you'll need to get permits and bids, and build the structure. While you can purchase a plan with nearly this level of detail, working with an architect gives you the advantage of being able to customize it to your needs, and it can cost only a few hundred dollars more than a generic plan you purchase. Orfield Design

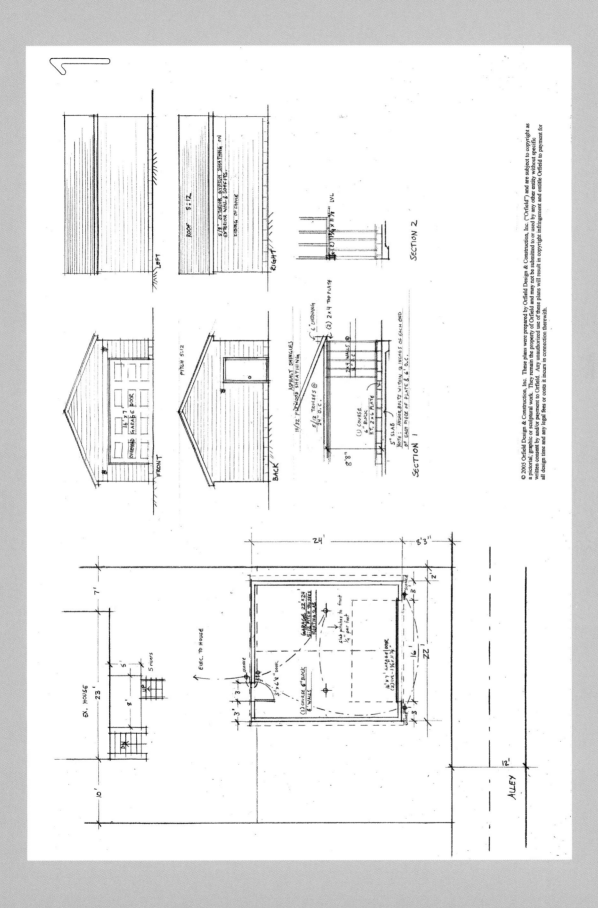

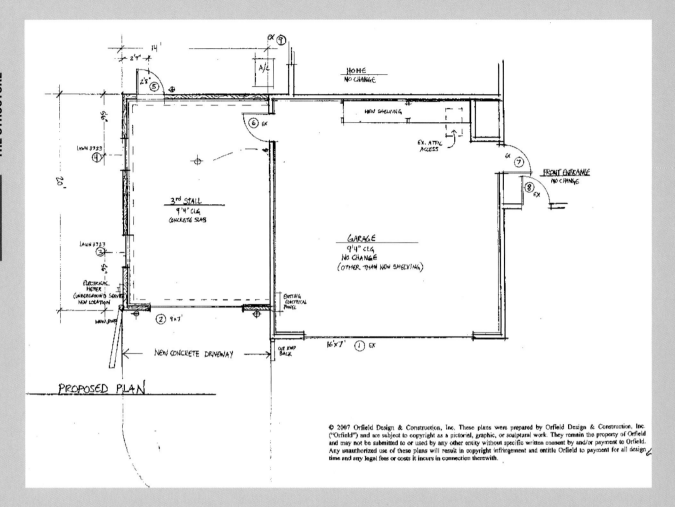

When you are doing a renovation or designing a custom garage, working with an architectural firm is a must. They will come out and measure your space, and their experience will most likely provide you with some new ideas on how to make the most of your space. Orfield Design

of Architects (www.aia.org), Architects USA (www.architectsusa.com), and BuilderSpace.com, which offer online architect finders that allow you to search by region and specialty.

Once you find a few who look like they meet your needs, spend some time meeting with them. Just as with your contractor, work with a person you enjoy and communicate effectively with rather than the lowest bidder. Rapport is important to getting the building you want!

Once you've done your research on what you want from your garage and have found an architect who is a good fit, you can get started. The process typically begins with a walk-around of your property in

which basic parameters are discussed. The architect will take some basic measurements and get an idea of what you want.

One key thing here is to clearly explain what you want and listen to what the architect suggests. They do this every day and will most likely offer some ideas you haven't considered. Make the most of your investment by taking advantage of their expertise.

After that, plans will be drawn up for you to inspect. Initially, these are typically rough drawings followed by detailed plans created once you have settled on the design. These plans will allow you to get bids from contractors and, if you are doing much of the work yourself, apply for permits at city hall.

Above: *The inside of a steel building can be finished as lavishly as any other. This space houses a car collection in a renovated warehouse.*

Left: *Lofts are an effective way to add recreational or business space to your garage. John Goodman's shop and garage houses his exceptional collection of Corvettes, Ferrari race cars, and a few other interesting machines.*

continued from page 33

Opposite: *This is another effective use of a steel building, which houses Crossroads Performance—a shop specializing in motorcycle speed parts—as well as the home of owner Mark Triebold. The walls are laced with windows to allow natural light into the building and give it a more open feel.*

expect to have to paint it every few years and to deal with rot and weathering.

Avoid synthetic stucco and wood-composite siding, which are prone to rot and are the most problematic siding types available.

 Siding is another area where it's tough to scrounge, scrape, or save, but you do have a couple of options. One is to gather a crew and side the garage yourself. If your structure is fairly low, siding is not rocket science. You'll want at least two guys to do this, and maybe four. Plus, you'll need ladders or preferably scaffolding to do the work on the higher walls.

For the real bargain-basement deal, find a place that sells reclaimed home-building materials (often called "re-use centers"). You can probably find a pile of siding big enough to slap on your shack for a price that is attractive. Who knows, you might get lucky and find some great cedar siding there. It doesn't cost anything to look.

Roofing

Once you select the design of your garage (see above) and, with it, the pitch of the roof, you only have a few decisions to make regarding the roof. The key one is the type of roofing material.

Again, if you are matching the house, it's not much of a decision: put on the same stuff that's on your house.

Whether or not you are matching your house, odds are you are going to use shingles, but there are some other types of roofing worth consideration. Tile and slate are gorgeous, durable, and outrageously expensive. Metal is an interesting option that looks great, particularly on barn-type structures. In the rain, they also result in a lovely drumming noise that I really enjoy, and they won't light on fire even if the neighbor's house is casting armloads of sparks on it.

Shingles are made of asphalt and have either an organic or fiberglass base. The fiberglass variety is more fire-resistant, cheaper, and more commonly used than the organic ones. Bear in mind that the organic-based shingles are an old design, not a new product designed to be more earth-friendly.

Be sure to use shingles that meet the standards of the American Society for Testing and Materials (ASTM), as not all of them do. Look for fiberglass shingles that are ASTM D-3462 rated; organic shingles should be rated ASTM D-225.

Shingles are also rated by fire resistance, and the best of the bunch are rated Class A, while the lowest acceptable rating is Class C. Look for the Class A variety. If you live

in Southern California, maybe you should consider metal, slate, or tile roofing.

If you live in a warm, humid climate, you may need to use shingles made with zinc- or copper-coated ceramic granules to protect against the algae.

 Cheapskates, here's a great place to save money. Shingling is hard work and requires some special ladders, not to mention the fact that you have to lug those heavy packets of shingles up to the roof. The work, however, is relatively simple to do, particularly if you can recruit a couple of your friends to help out. By doing the shingling yourself, you can save good money that you can turn around and spend on your garage lift or a new motorcycle.

The Garage Door

OK, so this isn't exactly an addition, but it is important. The first issue here is height. The standard garage door height is 7 feet to accommodate production vehicles. One of the tallest production vehicles is the Ford Excursion at 6 feet, 8 inches. This leaves 4 inches of clearance when it passes through a standard door. That's pretty tight and doesn't allow space for a ski rack.

An 8-foot door will buy some extra space for larger vehicles, and if you want to park your 16-foot covered snowmobile trailer, semitractor, or monster truck in the garage, you'll have to consider an even taller door.

If you don't have to make your garage ceiling higher than 9 feet, don't do it just to add space. The additional material and labor costs to make a garage taller than 9 feet are significant, and it's more expensive to heat and cool. Also, the space that is added is not as easy to use as additional width or a second floor. You simply build taller walls, which means that any shelving or cabinets you place in the top of that space will be hard to reach. If your lot allows it, building out will add space more cheaply than raising the height of your ground-floor ceiling.

Garage door width is another consideration. The standard two-car width is 18 feet, which works fine for parking two cars. For two trucks, it's a little tight. In three-car (or more) spaces, a second, smaller door is a nice option to consider. Also, if you are putting a workshop in an extra-deep garage, consider putting a small overhead door in the back. This is a great way to access motorcycles, lawn mowers, and other smaller equipment.

Garage doors vary a ton in price and material. You can purchase everything from steel to wood and even plastic. Wooden doors are gorgeous, expensive, and heavy (meaning they require more elaborate support and openers). They also tend to have shorter warranties than steel.

Steel doors work fine and are more economical. They are available in single-, double-, and triple-layer versions. The single-layer door is just a sheet of steel and is fine for an unheated, unattached garage. Steel doors can also be purchased with wood overlays, which provide the look of wood with the R-value (insulative property) and lighter weight of a steel door.

Bear in mind that you are going to want an insulated door if you live in a colder climate. The garage door is a huge part of your garage wall, and if you put on a cheap door with a low R-value, you are going to lose a lot of heat. This is where the double- and triple-layer doors are good. The best R-value comes from a triple-layer door with two sheets of steel wrapped around a foam core. Look for a door with core that is foamed-in polyurethane rather than injected polystyrene. Good doors give you an R-value of 8 to 11.

Note that the better steel doors have 24-gauge (or heavier) steel paneling, baked-on primer, polyester top coats, and at least a 10-year warranty.

 One interesting development is the PVC (polyvinyl chloride) garage door, which is lighter than steel is impervious to rust and rot, and comes with a 20-year warranty.

Finally, note that there are doors available that roll up. These can save a ton of space, as you eliminate the need for a long track running along the ceiling.

The Garage Door Opener

Cheapskates, it's hardly worth your time to scrounge up some used piece-of-junk garage door opener or to make your own by jury-rigging a chainsaw motor and the belt pulleys off a wrecked Rototiller. Just drag that checkbook out of your tight little back pocket and pony up. The good news? You can get a good-quality 1/2-horsepower opener with a keypad and a couple of remote controls for about $150.

Note that you'll need at least a 1/2-horsepower motor for a double door. The larger 3/4-horsepower units are needed for extra-large doors and a bit of happy overkill for double doors—the larger motor won't work as hard and will last longer.

Garage door openers are available with chain-, belt-, screw-, jackshaft-, and computer-controlled direct-drive electric motors that lift the door up. Chain-drive units are the most popular units out there and are priced between $100 and $200.

The belts are quieter than chains and are priced nearly identically to the chain-drive units.

Screw-drive units are a little more rugged than chain-drive openers, but are also slower to open than other types and are slightly more expensive. Expect to pay $150 to $200.

 Jackshaft-drive garage openers put the mechanism off to the side and maximize space in your garage. Computer-controlled mechanisms are a fairly recent development that mounts the opener on the wall above the door, saving space with a compact unit that mounts nearly flush to the wall. A direct-drive electric motor opens the door, and no chains or belts are needed.

Garage door openers will have an infrared sensor at the bottom of the door. If that beam is crossed while the door is closing, it will automatically reverse and open. Also, most of the openers on the market use a technology that changes the code each time you use the opener to prevent thieves from stealing your code.

Another way to create an attractive interior layout is to subdivide the space with walls and doorways. SwissTrax

Note that most openers are available with a battery backup so that the garage door will open even if the power is out. Depending on the brand, these can often be retrofitted if you decide you want one later. Also, a variety of security systems are available. One of the more interesting is a keypad that will open the door when a recognized fingerprint is swiped over it.

There are also other available safety features. Skylink, for one, offers an opener equipped with a carbon monoxide detector. If the levels of CO become too high, the door automatically opens. This unit can also automatically close the door if it is open after a preset amount of time. A company called Xceltronix offers a device that will automatically close your garage door after a preset time.

 Installing a garage door is one of those projects not recommended for the homeowner. It is heavy, uses powerful torsion springs that are dangerous to work with, and requires precise adjustment to function correctly. In addition, if you need to repair the tracks or springs, parts are not easily available to the homeowner. Hire a pro, expect to pay too much, and spend your time on other pursuits.

Second Floor

Adding a second floor to your garage is an economical way to create space in your home. The second floor won't add all that much relative cost to your new garage, and you will have an area that is great for storage or to finish into a game room, studio, or office. Just be warned—if you finish it too nicely, you may never make it back into your house!

This is also a good option to consider if you live on a small urban lot. Another interesting option is designing a building with a flat roof that you can use as a deck or patio.

A key to economical second-floor space is the trusses, which are cut so that you have space inside. If you use a fairly steep-pitched roof along with just a few extra feet in height, you'll have plenty of usable space upstairs.

Your contractor can help with this. Mine was able to add a second floor for only a few thousand dollars. I finished the floor and did all the insulation, which saved me a lot of money (which I spent on other goodies).

Before you get too caught up in the idea of a second floor, though, be sure to check your local building ordinances—some towns have fixed residential height restrictions and/or relative height restrictions that stipulate your garage can't be taller than your house.

If you add a second floor, you'll need a stairway. If you plan to use the floor as a living space, you'll need an outside entrance (i.e., exterior staircase) to meet most building codes.

For interior access to your upstairs, you can purchase a simple fold-down ladder for less than $150. These are fine for getting into a crawlspace you hardly ever access, and not much more. Second floors that have significant storage space are best accessed by a full stairway. I put in a fold-down ladder and curse the thing nearly every time I haul down the camping or motorcycle gear I store up there. Spend the money to put in a full staircase, even if you are a cheapskate.

Walk-In Door Options

Interior doors are designed to be used inside the structure, between rooms, while exterior doors have insulation and can be used in entry doorways. Doors between the garage and any living spaces often need to be exterior quality or at least fireproof. Check your local building codes to be sure about this point.

Before buying a door, make sure you have the right swing (left or right) to match the traffic flow in your garage.

You will want a prehung door if you do the installation yourself. These come from the factory set in a frame that you tip into a rough opening in the wall. Cheapskates, don't be afraid of hanging doors, but bear in mind there is more to it than just nailing it into place. You need to adjust how it fits in the opening with shims so that it opens and closes perfectly. You can find good instructions for this online. This is a task that can save you a little money, if you are so inclined.

Doors are available made of steel, wood, and fiberglass. They can be found with windows, panels, and all kinds of fancy trim. You can spend thousands on an elaborately finished door or less than $100 on a cheap solid-steel door that will work just fine for the garage and provide just as much, if not more, security. Cheapskates, this is a good place to save some money—low-cost doors will let you in just as effectively as those high-end doors.

Opposite: On interior walls, windows and doors with windows can give a space a more open feel. Don't forget to budget for these when you get bids on the garage.

Windows

When you are designing the structure, placement of windows will determine what it's like to be inside your new building. Windows simply make your garage a more pleasant place to spend time. Bear in mind that garage windows do have the problem of letting prying eyes look into your space. If you store valuable vehicles and tools in the garage and want to have some windows, consider high windows or cheap window coverings so that your valuable machinery is not visible to every neighborhood kid slinking around your house while you are away.

Be sure to place windows to take advantage of exterior light sources (i.e., north-facing windows or windows blocked by trees or other large objects obviously won't let in a lot of natural light). This will brighten up the space, and you will require less artificial lighting during the day.

Garage windows usually are not a place to save lots of money. For a space you are going to spend considerable time in, windows add a lot to the ambience and will keep you from getting the mole mentality that emerges if you work all day in your garage without seeing any daylight.

A good brand of window will last longer, insulate better, and work more smoothly than cheapos. If you aren't going to open and close the windows often and the building doesn't need to be tightly insulated, by all means go with bargain windows, but don't be surprised when the mechanisms jam.

If insulation is a factor in your structure, look for Energy Star–badged windows. Energy Star ratings are given out by the Department of Energy to products that exhibit energy-efficient qualities.

Cheapskates, you can find windows and doors at your local re-use center. If you want something cool and old for a reasonable price, this is one option. Likewise, if you are looking for a steel door for $25, well, this is your place to look.

Dormers and Skylights

If you opt for a second floor, dormers are a good way to make that space more useful. They are also good-looking
continued on page 46

Following pages: Another consideration that's easy to forget when budgeting is the landscaping and exterior spaces. Particularly when you are dealing with small lots, look for ways to use your exterior space as efficiently as your interior space. DiGiacomo Homes & Renovation

continued from page 42

and can help your garage match your home's style. Dormers are not terribly economical, however. Expect to pay at least $1,000 or more to add a small dormer; costs go up rapidly from that point for larger ones that add significant space.

Skylights are a great way to let light into a second floor, particularly if you want that to be a usable space and decide against dormers. Check the appendix for references to places to find skylights.

Interior Finish Work

Once the structure is up, you are probably going to want to finish off the inside. This topic is gone over in detail in later chapters. At this point of your process, just be sure to budget according to your intentions for floor coverings, interior walls, workbenches, insulation, and ceiling and wall coverings.

Installing these additions is a great way for the reasonably handy homeowner to save some money. Subcontractors can do all this work, but you will pay significant labor costs.

Aprons, Walkways, and Landscaping

Finally, be sure to budget for the exterior finish work necessary to complete your project. You'll likely want a concrete apron in front of the garage and may need new walkways and lawn installed after the job is complete.

With a drive, be sure to carefully map out where it is going to go, perhaps even staking out the outline of the garage and driveway. Walk around the outline and drive down it. Is there enough room to get into the driveway? Is there enough room between the house and garage? Where would you put a patio? Are you in compliance with setbacks and other ordinances? Once the concrete company pours the slab for your garage, the time for you to make changes will have passed!

When the time comes to finish your drive, you have a number of options. You may be able to make do with a gravel drive in rural parts of the country, but most municipalities require some kind of finished driveway. The most economical option is chip seal, asphalt with gravel pressed into it. This requires some maintenance as you have to add gravel and sealant periodically, and finding a company that will install it can be a challenge. Your building codes may not allow this type of surface, as well, so it isn't a practical choice for most of us.

Asphalt is easily available and relatively economical. The drawbacks with asphalt are that you'll need to apply fresh sealant every three years or so, and in hot climates asphalt can become soft and sticky. On hot days, you cannot park motorcycles on the surface, as the sidestand will

dig in and scar the asphalt. Even leaving your car parked on it can make indentations. On the other hand, a good asphalt driveway that is well maintained should last between 25 and 30 years.

 Concrete is the longest-lasting choice for a driveway and typically costs twice as much as asphalt. In the long term, concrete is the best choice, both aesthetically and economically. You won't have to seal concrete, ever, and you can have patterns printed, dyed, or painted on the surface. True, concrete will develop hairline cracks over the years, but you can avoid large cracks by having a properly compacted gravel or Class 5 base installed beneath it. (This is no different for asphalt: the quality of your base will determine the stability of your drive.)

BUILDING THE STRUCTURE

You've found architectural plans and know the specific modifications you want to make to them. You have chosen the spot where the garage will be built and have decided on the details of what you want inside the garage. It's time to get down to it and get this thing built.

If you are building it yourself, get the slab poured and start stocking up on beer with which to bribe your hammer-worthy friends for help.

And, of course, you have to line up your general contractor or subcontractors to do all the work you aren't going to do yourself.

General Contractors

Most people use a general contractor to build their garage. The typical contractor has a crew that does the basic carpentry (framing, siding, and roofing) and uses subcontractors for the rest of the work.

Many architectural firms will also do all of your contracting for you. This is a good route if you want a turnkey operation, but you'll probably pay a bit more than you would with a one-man shop.

These guys are essentially job bosses, and working with one of them is the simplest way to get anything built. You talk with one person who coordinates all the details (typically including getting inspections and making sure everything in the structure meets building codes). All you have to do is write a check.

As with any industry, there is a wide assortment of contractors out there. Most, but not all, are honest people who will treat you right. Ask around to see if you can get a recommendation for a good contractor. You can also find contractors in the Yellow Pages or online. Check to see if they belong to local industry groups. Ask for references.

This tuck-under garage (left and below) is an elaborate example of what you can do with a garage remodel. The owners worked with an architectural firm, Vujovich Design, to come up with a custom plan for the renovation. The renovated garage that results is nearly impossible to recognize. Living space and a new deck were added above the garage.
Both Vujovich Design

Next, get at least three bids for your job. In order to compare bids fairly, you will need a very detailed plan of the structure you have in mind. Do as much research as you can and then ask lots of questions of the contractors. How thick will the walls be? What kind of shingles will be used? Siding? Take notes.

When the bids come in, don't automatically take the lowest one. Compare the specs and talk to your references. If you get along well with the contractor, that's a plus. You are going to have to spend some time dealing with this person and probably make some decisions you'll make only a few times in your life. If you enjoy the person's company and trust them, the process will be much simpler and more fun to boot.

Even if you like the contractor, ask for references. Talk to some people who have worked with them so you know that they are capable of doing a good job. If the contractor refuses to give you references, don't walk away—run.

Also, bear in mind that you will get a lower price from a smaller outfit. A guy working out of his truck will charge less than an architectural firm. In general, though, you will get better service from larger outfits. They have more pull with subcontractors and can make sure everyone shows up when scheduled. During busy building times, this is an important factor, as getting an electrician or plumber to even show up can be difficult.

If your timeline isn't critical and you like the idea of working with a one-man or small-crew contractor, by all means save some money and go with them. Just be aware

of the compromises you will make when working with small firms.

When you decide on the contractor who offers a fair price, has good references, and is someone you trust, be prepared to wait awhile for their services, even if the housing market is slow. Good contractors are generally booked several months in advance.

Once you settle, be sure to put everything in writing. Good contractors have a contract that you sign, which lists what's included in the price, dates and amounts of payments, and terms and conditions for making changes or additions. Be sure the contractor is responsible for getting the necessary permits, and check that they are insured.

It Ain't Easy Being Green I: How to Build Green

What You'll Need: "Green" materials, common sense, a good contractor
Time: 1–8 hours
Tab: Modest initial investment and good long-term savings

Today, you don't have to look hard to find lots of references to "green" building materials. From garage doors made from recycled PVC (polyvinyl chloride) to shingles that contain recycled materials, there are myriad building products that appeal to this country's greener side.

Well, the fact of the matter is, most of the "green" building material bit is hype. The products are often much more expensive than the nonorganic stuff, and most people aren't willing to put up with 300 percent cost increases to feel better about themselves. In fact, most of us can't afford to spend that kind of money!

That's probably a relief to most of the gearheads in the world because we aren't known for being the most environmentally friendly sots in the world. But listen up, Mr. or Ms. Burning-Gas-Is-My-Favorite-Hobby: you can use some of the so-called green building tactics to your advantage.

A building that is energy efficient will save you heating dollars down the road and save a whale or two by minimizing how much energy your home uses. Spend a little more on windows and doors that seal tightly and insulate well. This is particularly important with garage doors in heated garages. An uninsulated garage door lets a significant volume of heat escape and will add to your heating costs significantly.

In addition, long-lasting, maintenance-free products will minimize the waste generated by your home. Cheap siding, for example, will most likely end up in a landfill 10 years down the road when you replace it because it's falling apart. The same is true for low-quality shingles.

If you spend a lot of time in your garage and need to heat it full-time, consider in-floor heating. This system is very efficient and cost-effective,

particularly when compared to the gas heaters that hang from your ceiling. The gas heaters are great if you warm up the garage for a few weekends each winter, but they are horribly inefficient when used on an extended, regular basis.

A living space that uses water efficiently and has high-quality air is also considered a "green building." A water-saving toilet is one garage-builder option. Air quality is a bit tougher, particularly if you are prone to spending your evenings in the garage revving your big-block Chevy to the moon. (Note from our lawyers: FOR GOD'S SAKE, DON'T DO THIS.)

Check with your local governmental agency to see if there are any benefits to building green. Several states have programs that offer tax credits, special mortgage rates, and improved utility and insurance rates for approved green builders.

Another way you can be green without losing respect for yourself is to recycle all the old materials that come out of your garage. If you tear down an old garage, consider donating the doors, windows, siding, and lumber to a re-use center. You can also post that you have material to give away at Web sites such as Craigslist and Freecycle, and people may just show up to haul the old stuff away for you.

Building green means more than using recycled materials—the best green techniques take into consideration how the owner's activities affect the world around them. This garage was designed to funnel car-wash runoff into a dry well and rain garden covered with recycled mulch rather than into the nearby Mississippi River. Paul Markert/DiGiacomo Homes & Renovation, Inc.

A kit is a garage option for handy homeowners. A good kit comes with detailed instructions and all the materials you need to put up your own garage. You'll need to recruit some help to raise the roof and walls. This garage was built from a kit supplied by Shelter Kit. *Shelter Kit*

Kits

One option for the do-it-yourselfer is a garage kit. These are available at home-supply retailers such as Home Depot and Menards and from smaller custom builders like Summerwood Products and Shelter Kit. The kit will include all the construction materials you need to build the structure, along with instructions of varying detail. The prices for these kits can be quite attractive, with complete garages selling for $5,000 and up. Note that some of these kits can be purchased completely assembled, and a truck will come by and drop your new garage off.

If you go with a kit, you'll need to get your own permits, have a slab poured, and do the construction work yourself. Also, many kits come with minimal instructions, and the materials are generally bargain-basement quality.

The better kits from custom manufacturers like Summerwood and Shelter Kit cost between $10,000 and $30,000 and come with detailed instructions. Bear in mind that you need to be quite handy and have access to a small crew of people to build a kit garage.

 This is definitely a case where you are better off spending more money on a quality kit. The step-by-step instructions and available help from the company are worth the extra cost alone. If you don't need the instructions, you are better off stick-building the garage from scratch.

Companies like Shelter Kit will even build the kit to your specifications and prepare everything you need to apply for your permit.

Self-Contracting

One route to consider is self-contracting the project. This is ideal if you have a lot of time and energy to expend on the project. You also need to be very organized and detail oriented.

If these traits describe you, by all means do your own contracting. You'll have to line up several contractors to do the work, from pouring the slab to wiring electrics to running pipes.

You can find contractors in the Yellow Pages or in the ads in your local community newspaper. As with a general contractor, ask for references. But remember: because you will offer the contractor only this one job, you won't have much pull. If one of the contractor's bigger customers calls and demands that a job of theirs takes precedence over yours, your project is almost guaranteed to be delayed.

Self-contracting is also ideal if you can do some of the work yourself. If you are able to do the framing and roofing, for example, and then hire out the concrete, electrical, and siding, self-contracting might be a great option and an obvious way to save money.

If you are truly interested in taking this route, I highly recommend *Be Your Own House Contractor* by Carl Heldman. I read this book before doing my own garage and was able to determine that self-contracting was not for me. In general, if you have a very busy life or are not terribly well organized or detail oriented, you might be better off with a general contractor.

CHAPTER 2
THE FLOOR PLAN

Your building is up, and it's time to think through your layout. The key here is figuring out what you want to do in the garage and then adapting the space to those needs. If you happen to be overly anal retentive, those tendencies can serve you well. If you're not fastidious by nature, for once in your life, do just a little planning. Buy some graph paper, sharpen your crayon, and spend a little time drawing out what you think might work.

This is your work palace. You want it to be right. The first thing to consider is the type of space you want or need based on the kind of use you anticipate.

If this is just a place to park and show off your toys, plan accordingly. If you want workspaces, draw them out and allow a bit more space than you think you'll need. Spaces that look pretty generous on graph paper seem to shrink a bit in reality.

Do you want to have a space to hang out with your buddies? Allow a little room for some chairs and maybe an old couch (and a fridge—one of the essential garage accessories).

If you need office space or a game room, draw it in. A workable office requires very little space: an enclosed office measuring 8x8 feet is big enough for a desk and a printer.

When planning, remember that any space that you spend a lot of time in will benefit greatly from some natural light. Windows are relatively cheap when you are building a new space.

Line up windows with your exterior light sources. This will brighten up the space, and you will require less artificial lighting during the day.

If you are completely incapable of planning (you know who you are), you have a couple of options. You can bribe someone you know who is good at it to help you draw it up. Or do as Mark Triebold at Crossroads Performance did—just lay it out as you go.

Mark has a motorcycle customization shop in Somerset, Wisconsin. He put up a large steel building and filled the interior with a retail shop, work area, and living area.

"I see spaces well," Mark says. "I just laid out walls the way I thought it would work."

His workspace is amazingly usable, with workbenches, an area with bike lifts, and a conference room and lunchroom all tucked inside.

Crossroads Performance is a machine shop specializing in motorcycle speed parts as well as customization. Mark Triebold, the owner, laid out his space as he built it. Most of us don't possess that kind of eye, but his space turned out nicely.

Bear in mind that Mark has the right kind of mind for this. If you are spatially challenged, experiment with different layouts on paper, and you may find that your end result works quite well.

Another option to keep your space flexible is to give yourself as much open space as you can practically afford (and need—more for cars and trucks, less for motorcycles or bicycles). This is particularly useful if you are not planning to add interior walls. Then, equip your garage with rolling toolboxes, benches, and work stands. This will allow you to adjust the setup depending on the project, and you'll discover new and innovative ways to use the space.

One thing you may have to consider is power sources—you are going to have to put in the electrical early if you cover the walls. Always put in more power outlets than you think you can use—one double outlet for every 6 feet of floor space is a good rule of thumb. For workbench areas, place four-outlet power strips at bench height (about 48 inches off the floor) and space them 4 feet apart over the bench. See the section on electrical considerations for more information on this topic.

FINISHING THE WALLS

 If your garage isn't heated, the simplest option is to leave bare stud walls. In fact, I recommend this, as it allows you to adjust the electrical routing, air lines, and layout after using the space for a bit. And open stud walls can be turned into storage shelves and racks very simply.

Many garages in northern climates are insulated and sheetrocked. Use heavier grade 5/8-inch sheetrock, as it will stand up to dings and dents a bit better.

Another option is to cover the bottom portion of the wall in metal. Diamond plate looks particularly good and is durable enough to handle the bumps, bangs, and even the occasional part that springs off your project (or is thrown across the room). Metal coatings are also a nice addition if you plan to have a hose in the garage—metal will handle any overspray much better than sheetrock.

FLOOR COATINGS

Bare concrete is vulnerable to stains, and dirt tends to cling to it over time. A coating makes it easier to clean and maintain, is resistant to stains, and looks great. Did I mention how nice it looks?

Opposite: You can, of course, go completely over the top with your garage's finish. This is not really a working space, but it is an exceptional showpiece.
Washingtonspaces.com

Be aware that a joke being passed around the Internet insinuates that the guy with the color-coded garage floor is a deluded yuppie, while real wrenches work on bare concrete in a dingy room too dirty for rats (and are terminally single).

 Mr. Cheapskate, you may or may not be terminally single, but you will probably be content with bare concrete. It works just fine if you don't mind some cracks and stains.

Before covering the floor with paint (or tile or mats; see below) you need to repair any cracks or crumbling concrete. A number of excellent products are available that involve everything from simply chipping out the loose concrete and pouring in a fresh layer of Portland cement to using bonding agents that literally glue the patch in place. However you patch it, make sure your garage floor is flat and smooth before applying a new coating or tile.

If you want to paint your garage floor, you'll find a dizzying array of products to choose from. The most popular method is to paint the floor with one of the many DIY kits on the market that use epoxy, polyurethane, or polyurea paint. These paints bond tightly to the floor and are durable enough to survive the wear and tear of vehicles and the inevitable oil and antifreeze spills. The biggest drawbacks cited with these products are the hassle of applying the coating and the fact that some of them can be slick when the surface gets damp. You can counteract this by using a nonskid additive to provide some grit to the final coat.

Most of the kits you'll find at your local home improvement store use epoxy, and it's a reasonable choice to coat your floor. Epoxy requires three days to dry, and the floor needs to be at 50 degrees or warmer to apply it. The tensile strength of an epoxy coating is just over 3,000 psi, about half that of polyurethane or polyurea. You can purchase a kit to cover 600 square feet (a 24x24-foot garage) for about $300.

Polyurethane is another type of garage-floor coating, and most of these products provide a tensile strength of about 5,000 psi (better than epoxy, but less than polyurea). The abrasion resistance is the lowest of the three options, and it takes longer to set up. A kit to cover 600 square feet with a polyurethane top coat will cost you about $450.

Polyurea is a newer product that has been used for commercial applications and has recently been made available for consumer use. The product cures quite quickly—you can coat your garage in the morning and drive on it the next day. Also, it gives off very little chemical odor, will not yellow over time, and can be applied to wood. The tensile strength (6,000 psi) and abrasion resistance of polyurea is the highest of the three, and the cost is comparable.

Draw Your Floor Plan

Tools and Supplies: Pencil, paper, ruler, measuring tape
Time: 10 minutes–?
Tab: $0–$250 (for design software package)

Let's say you are going to want space for three cars and two motorcycles, a workbench with a grinder and a welder, and a game room. And down the road you might want to add an air compressor and a parts-washing bench.

The key is to use your space efficiently. You can lay it out ad hoc, of course, or use the flexible workspace mentioned in this chapter.

The best path to efficiency, however, is to carefully plan out your space on paper. You can use graph paper and hand-draw the plan, or you can use a software package such as ConceptDraw.

Carefully draw out the walls for your garage. Now take that drawing to a copy machine and make a bunch of photocopies.

Now, you can start doodling. Draw walls in different spots, move around your work areas, and place cars, motorcycles, jet skis, and other toys in the garage.

Experiment until you are happy with the result. And don't hesitate to show off your drawing to friends, relatives, and the people in your car or motorcycle club. You'll often find that even your buddy who can barely spell his own name will have a decent suggestion to make your plan perfect.

This drawing is an excellent thing to show an architect, if you use one. Using space is their profession, and they will undoubtedly have some suggestions to help you improve the layout of your garage.

Above: *Metal siding was used to cover the stud walls in the Crossroads Performance building, giving the garage a pleasingly industrial look.*

Opposite: *This garage uses top-of-the-line SwissTrax tile flooring, custom cabinets, and narrow windows to make an attached garage something special.* SwissTrax

Whichever coating you choose, all come in a variety of colors, and the final coat can be brightened up by adding colored chips. A few companies have chips that glow in the dark or light up under black light. A more useful chip option is the nonskid variety, which will help keep the floor from becoming too slick.

The color-chipped coatings look great and are easy to customize. Check out the custom mix simulator at the Original Chip Company's Web site to see how various paint color and chip color mixes look.

Note that the better brands finish the process by applying a clear top coat that protects the floor from staining caused by general wear and tear. Avoid the kits that don't use a clear top coat.

Following pages: *Another example of warehouse space, but this on a little grander scale. The tile floor separates the space into parking slots and aisles.*

Coating your garage floor is an ideal project for Mr. or Ms. Cheapskate. It's easy to do and takes no more than a day even for a large surface. See the sidebar for specific instructions.

RUBBER MATS

You can purchase a variety of mats to cover your garage floor. They come in large sheets and in square tiles, and thicknesses vary from 0.055 inch to 0.085 inch. These are a nice solution for older floors, as they cover stains, cracks, and so on. Installation is a snap.

You can also purchase sheets to protect the floor underneath your motorcycle or car. This works well for older vehicles that tend to drip fluids. A ribbed mat under your car is a good choice in northern climates, as it will catch the ice, snow, and salt dripping off your vehicle.

TILE

The easiest to install and most dynamic-looking durable garage flooring on the market is interlocking tile. The better brands can endure up to 5,120 psi, withstand 40,000-pound loads, and come with 12- or 15-year warranties. The tiles are made of plastic, recycled PVC, or polypropylene, and can be ordered in a wide variety of colors. If you

An effective workspace is not just good-looking, but useful. A long, narrow space is great if you have several automotive projects going at once.

dream of a four-color checkerboard floor in your garage, these tiles are the hot setup. You can find a slick floor designing palette at the SwissTrax and RaceDeck Web sites, where you can also choose from a rainbow of colors.

Tile is good-looking and easy to install, but it's not cheap. Cost for the material starts at about $4 per square foot, meaning that covering a 24x24-foot garage will cost you around $2,300.

You can also cover your floor in stone tile, which is a popular treatment for high-end display garages. Material costs alone for stone tile run $4 per square foot and up—expect to pay $10 or more per square foot to have stone tile installed.

 If you absolutely need that tiled look in your garage but don't want to spend a lot of dough, VCT (vinyl composition tile) is the hot setup for you, El Cheapo Grande.

VCT is designed for use in hospitals, schools, and other institutions that require cheap, durable flooring.

The tile comes in squares of various sizes. Some of it is available in more elaborate patterns, while the dirt-cheap varieties are available in solid colors only. You can buy VCT for about 75 cents per square foot, meaning you can do an average-sized two-car garage for less than $500 (just a few dollars more expensive than coating the floor with paint and much better-looking).

And don't forget to check out Craigslist before you buy the stuff new. Because the material is used in large industrial jobs, people end up with leftovers fairly regularly. I did a quick search and found a guy selling 4,000 square feet of VCT for $450.

No matter how cheap you are, don't use the bargain-priced peel-and-stick vinyl squares. These don't stay in place and will separate, peel, and look terrible after only a few years.

DRAINAGE

If you are building new, a floor drain is a great feature. It allows you to wash vehicles in your garage and wash down the floor. Instruct your contractor to make sure the floor

For storage/recreational space, an open floor plan works well. Bill Cotter's warehouse in Seattle is a good example. He uses rolling tool chests and parts carts so that he can work on his cars wherever he chooses.

Floor coatings add a lot of aesthetic value to your garage and make the floor easier to clean and more durable. This epoxy coating is the most common and one of the most economical. Note that polyurea coatings will likely replace epoxy due to their superior durability and much quicker drying times.

is properly sloped to the drain, and check with your local regulations concerning garage drains. You may have to tap into the city sewer system or build the drain field to code.

If you want to add a drain or think you might want to add water or sewer service to your garage, be sure to have the lines run when the structure is built.

DEALING WITH INSPECTIONS AND PERMITS

When building your garage, you are going to need to keep your city building inspector happy. Those of you in rural areas may be able to build whatever you like without a whole lot of interference from local government, but for most of us, city hall has a long list of building codes they expect you to obey.

First, you need to get the proper building permits. Doing just about anything to your urban home—building a deck, changing wiring, resurfacing a driveway, and siding your house—requires you to get a permit.

If you don't apply for your permits, the people down at city hall can and will make your life difficult (don't ask me how I know this). So find out what you need before you start that project and are later told that you can't do what you are doing and that you have to tear the whole damn thing out.

Your city hall's or county seat's Web site can be a great source for information about this. You can also stop in and pick up building-code sheets.

After your project is complete, you need to get it inspected. This entails spending more money, and the

Opposite above: *Tile flooring is the ultimate in terms of easy installation and durability. Tile is also the most expensive and the best-looking. This is a SwissTrax tile coating. They and the other reputable tile manufacturers allow you to custom-design your floor pattern and color. SwissTrax*

Opposite below: *Windows add immeasurably to any garage space and can be used to make your garage a much more pleasant place to spend time. RaceDeck*

people at city hall can direct you on how to make arrangements for an inspection once a particular project or phase is complete.

There's absolutely no way to cut corners here—if you skip inspections, you may not be able to sell your house.

If you are working with a contractor, you shouldn't need to worry about this. Good contractors handle all permits and inspections, and the really good ones have positive relationships with the local building inspectors and are familiar with code. Ask about that when considering which contractor to go with.

If your project is DIY, your best bet is to ask around. Ask your neighbors what they know, and do as much reading on the city's Web site as you can stand.

Once you have some familiarity with the code, stop down at city hall and talk with the inspector. Be polite and friendly and ask them what is needed. If you act like a nice guy, your odds of the inspector showing up and being understanding rather than troublesome will rise dramatically. This is a case where nice guys may not finish first, but they do have a better shot of getting their project approved without endless wrangling with city hall.

Coat Your Garage Floor

Supplies: Paint kit
Tools: Concrete grinder or acid-etching kit, Shop-Vac with long attachment, paint roller with 6-foot handle 3/8- and 1/4-inch rollers, roller pan, paint brushes, Squeegee
Time: 4–6 hours
Tab: $300–$800

The latest, greatest product on the market to coat garage floors is polyurea, which is more durable than any other floor paint and cures much more quickly, meaning you can have the job complete on Saturday and drive on the surface on Sunday (epoxy requires three or more days to properly cure). A few retailers had it available at press time. By the time you read this, this product should be commonly available. Expect to pay about $2 per square foot covered for this material.

Before you paint, clean the garage floor thoroughly with a 3-to-1 mixture of water and bleach. If you like to throw money away, use commercial garage-floor cleaner to do the same thing.

Rinse the whole floor clean with a hose or a pressure washer after that. Once you have the floor cleaned up, seal the cracks with a concrete-repair compound.

Concrete surfaces will need etching before you paint. To check if yours needs this, sprinkle some water on the surface. If the water is absorbed into the concrete quickly, no need for etching (new concrete floors often need etching). Use a commercial etching product, which is a liquid that literally deglazes your floor. Rinse the floor again after you etch.

Note that this floor was coated with polyurea, the most durable paint-on coating on the market. You can purchase this product from Rock Solid Flooring, Slide-Lok, and other retailers around the country.

The first step to prepping your floor is to prepare the concrete by roughing it up so the coating bonds to it. You can do this with liquid etcher, or you can use a diamond grinder, a machine that uses little grinding wheels to scratch the concrete.

Large diamond grinders can be rented at most tool rental places. This one is the WerkMaster Octi-Disc, which uses eight floating discs to grind the floor.

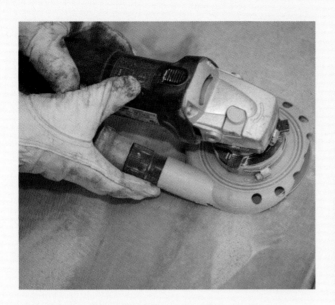

For areas that the big machine can't reach, you'll have to use a hand grinder equipped with a diamond-bladed concrete grinding disc. Be careful with the handhelds—you can create dips if you don't keep the grinder moving in a swirling motion.

After grinding is complete, vacuum the entire floor with a Shop-Vac to remove the concrete dust.

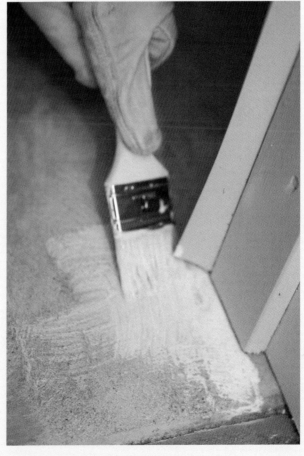

Above: The next step is to mix up your primer coat. A paint-mixing attachment on a drill works well. This syrupy, semiclear liquid sets up fairly quickly, so get it down as quickly as you can. **Right:** Paint around the edges with a brush before you do the middle of the floor.

This is a floor—use cheap rollers, brushes, and pans to apply the primer coat. You just need to cover the concrete with a clear skin. A 3/8-inch roller works well. Once the entire floor is coated, wait about 30 minutes before applying the next coat.

Next, mix your paint. These buckets with measurements on the side are handy for getting your ratios correct. Check in the kit for the proper mix ratios.

If you are using antislip additives or any tints, mix them in at this point.

To walk on the coated floor, strap these spikes (included in kit) to your shoes. Be careful on the freshly coated floor, as it will be slippery.

Roll on the paint coat and trim around the edges with a small brush.

The chip blend gives the floor a rich look and is simply tossed on top of the paint. Do this immediately after the paint is applied and still tacky.

The final clear coat is applied after the paint coat has dried for about 40 minutes. Spread this out with a squeegee.

Finish spreading out the top coat with a 1/4-inch roller. If you coated the floor with polyurea, let the floor dry for 24 hours and drive your car in. Epoxies will require three days or more to dry.

CHAPTER 3
POWER, LIGHT, AND HEAT

You're going to want electrical power in your garage. The key question is how much?

Most garages are fine with 50- or 100-amp service, but some do require more. If you intend to have heavy-load equipment such as welders or electric heaters, you'll need more amperage.

You'll find lots of confusing, complicated formulas out there to determine if you need 200-amp service in your garage. The best of those is Article 220 in the *National Electrical Code* book. You can buy the book online for about $70, and you may or may not be able to understand it. You can also buy a number of other equally expensive books that explain how to interpret the NEC book (and are probably still only comprehensible by electricians, engineers, and others in the industry).

If you are determined to do the math, try the *Audel Guide to the 2005 National Electrical Code* published by Paul Rosenburg. The book costs less than $20 and is designed to give electricians the information they need to follow the NEC.

You can also simply add up the requirements of all the things you intend to use in the garage (see sidebar). This is also pretty useful to figure out how to set up your breaker circuits.

That said, unless you use electric heat, a high-powered welder, or lots of computers in your garage, you probably don't need 200-amp service.

But consider this: it will cost anywhere from $2,000 to $4,000 to upgrade to 200-amp service down the road (depending on if you finish your walls and use wire that can carry the loads). If you install 200-amp service when you build the garage, it's maybe another $500.

If you have any reason to suspect you might need more power later on, spend the extra money up front. In the garage, there is no such thing as too much power.

Another consideration is the placement of outlets and light switches. Look carefully at your power needs and put in about twice as many outlets as you think you'll need.

continued on page 71

A large facility like this is going to have dramatic power requirements. Even a smaller garage can benefit from ample power—consider installing 200-amp service in your garage if you intend to run a lot of equipment.

This overhead bank of covered lights provides great light, which owner Kevin Manley uses to detail his collector Mustangs.

Calculate for Garage Power Needs

To calculate the maximum electrical power requirements of your garage, locate the power-rating label on your garage equipment and total the watts or amperes. For incandescent lights, use the wattage rating on the bulbs, and for fluorescent, find the number on the fixture's label. Convert all power requirements to amperes by dividing the number of watts by 110. The ampere is a more convenient measure for this purpose because circuit breakers are rated in amperes.

Next, compare your calculated amperes to the circuit breaker rating marked on the front or side of the circuit breaker handle at the electrical panel. You don't want to overload the circuit breaker's rating.

continued from page 66

Around the garage, a double bank every 8 feet is a decent rule of thumb.

Over my workbench, I put in two banks of four outlets. All are full right now, and I wish I had two more banks of four. Once you start plugging in lights, power-pack chargers, compressors, grinders, and all the other tools you want on the bench, you run out.

I consider 12 to 16 outlets about right for a serious workbench and recommend stringing them out in a line of singles that run on the bottom of the bench. Of course, if you do put in too few (as I did), a power strip can save the day.

If you plan to put in a welder, consider a 220-volt outlet. You might want two if you aren't sure where you want to put your welder.

ADDITIONAL WIRING CONSIDERATIONS

While running the electrical, also consider phone and cable television lines. Having a phone in the garage can be helpful, and who doesn't want to be able to watch the race

continued on page 75

The overhead lighting in this room is primarily screw-in bulbs. The light output is fairly low, which allows the owner's collection of neon signs to stand out. In a working garage, you'll want better light than this.

Upgrade Your Garage's Lighting

Supplies: Raptor RAP1 T5/HO (high-output) Luminaire (or other new lighting units), 2 1/2–inch wood screws, wire nuts, pigtail
Tools: Phillips screwdriver
Time: 1 hour
Tab: $40–$170 per light

If you work in your garage after dark, good lighting is crucial. Not only is it helpful to be able to see what you are working on, but bright lighting makes your garage seem brighter and more inviting, while dim lighting makes the place seem like a dungeon rather than your wrench-spinning palace. Also, good lighting is just safer.

Most garages are equipped with cheap overhead lighting—either bare bulbs or cheap fluorescents—that put out just enough light to drive in the family car and bolt inside to catch the latest episode of *American Idol*. If you prefer to spend your time wrenching rather than molding the couch to your backside, a lighting upgrade will improve your experience.

In this case, a set of rock-bottom-priced fluorescents were lighting a 24x28 garage and were never anything more than dim.

The replacement units are Raptor 1 high-output T5 fluorescent overhead lights made by The Light Edge that put out 5,000 lumens (compared to 600 watts from a light bulb). The ballasts fire even in temperatures down to -20 degrees Fahrenheit, the lamps are rated to last 24,000 hours, and the housings are one-piece extruded aluminum. Cost is high for these, at $160 per 4-foot bank, and you can purchase them only through R. E. Williams.

These lights are one of the most powerful garage lights you can find—they are even, color correct (important for painting and staining), and very, very bright. And, as promised, they don't buzz or flicker.

Left: *These $10 specials bought at a local home improvement store put out dim light and flickered, buzzed, and didn't light up in the cold.* **Above:** *The first step is to remove the old units by pulling off the plastic covers and removing the bulbs with a twist. Note that fluorescent bulbs run cool and can be pulled out with the lights on.*

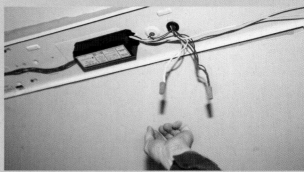

Once the bulbs are out, be sure to cut the power to the lighting unit. The easiest way to do this is to switch off the breaker. Make sure that you have no power at the unit before proceeding! Back out any screws holding the ballast cover in place and pull it off.

Once the ballast cover is off, you can pull off the wire nuts and disconnect the power. Then remove the screws holding the unit to the ceiling and pull it down.

Most overhead lights come from the factory with three bare wires protruding from the top or end of the unit. You can either hardwire this into your garage or attach a pigtail so you can plug the unit into an outlet. To attach the pigtail, remove the cover from the unit.

The slim fluorescent tubes need to be removed from this unit to wire the pigtail.

Left: The reflector has to be removed to access the wiring. Loosen the two screws holding it in and lift it out. Right: This pigtail was purchased at a home improvement store for less than $10.

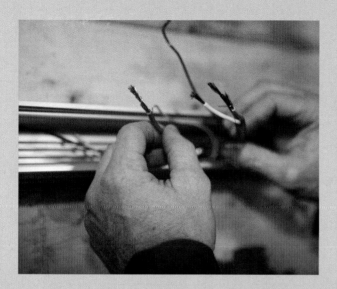

Twist the black, white, and green wires together (black to black, white to white, etc.). The green wire is the ground wire. Use wire nuts to secure the connections. Strip the wires 1/2-inch so that no bare wires protrude from the wire nuts. Bare wires are bad—if you see any, either cut them shorter or cover the bare wire with electrical tape.

Once the wires are connected, tuck the pigtail into the housing.

Above: These Raptor-brand units can be hung with light chain or with the clips seen here. Fasten the clips to the ceiling by sinking a 2 1/2-inch wood screw into a stud. Don't try to hang these things with sheetrock anchors—the lights require the support of a screw biting into solid wood! **Above right:** If you are using outlets to power your new overhead lights, wire in the outlets and cover (see next sidebar) and then snap the lighting unit into the clips. Make sure the clips snap completely over the edges of the housing. You can slide the light in the clips to position it perfectly. **Right:** Plug it in, and you have new lighting in the garage.

continued from page 71

while working on their car or bike on Sunday afternoon?

Note that electrical work in a garage is not beyond the reach of the DIY enthusiast. The key is to get some advice from someone who knows the codes in your area. The actual work isn't hard, but knowing the rules and regulations is tricky. If you tackle this aspect of your garage, get one of the good books out there on the subject, such as *The Complete Guide to Home Wiring* or *Wiring a House* by Rick Caldwell. You can find several good articles online.

If you are going to eventually sheetrock the inside of the garage, all the wires need to run inside the studs so that you have flush surfaces to screw on your sheetrock. If not, you can run wires across faces, but do so only in places that don't see much wear.

Consider paying an experienced electrician for a couple hours of labor. You could have them come to your garage and give you some pointers beforehand and stop by afterward to make sure you have everything up to code.

Speaking of code, most cities require an electrical permit and inspection for wiring a new building or upgrading existing wiring. Consult your local city inspector on how to go about filing for a permit (before you do the work) and getting it inspected when you are finished.

LIGHTING

Lighting needs to be ample, well placed, and adequate to work at the temperatures that are typical in your garage. Starting with overhead lighting, you want the lights spaced out enough to provide decent lighting.

The most basic overhead option is the single outlet with a bare bulb. These work just fine. They won't provide brilliant light, but they are dirt cheap. Space them about one every 6 feet, and you'll have plenty of light.

The next step up the rung is fluorescent-tube lighting. These range from $10 to $170 per fixture. Fixtures come in 4-, 6-, and 8-foot lengths and typically have two bulbs. With fluorescent lighting, the 4-foot banks are a good choice because the bulbs are much easier to handle.

 I can tell you from experience (see sidebar) that you get what you pay for. The low-end banks will provide light—it's true—but the light is weak, they light slowly (or not at all) if the temperature drops below about 55 degrees, and they emit an annoying buzz. Honestly, I think the bare light bulbs are a better choice if you are going to economize on your lighting system.

A good rule of thumb for garage lighting is one 8-foot bank per vehicle space. You can also go by kilowatts per square foot, with one kilowatt per square foot providing reasonable lighting and two kilowatts being on the bright side. You can find a calculator for this at General Electric's lighting Web site.

Fluorescent tubes come in two sizes: T8 (1.0-inch-diameter tubes) and T12 (1.5-inch tubes). The T8s are more expensive but better suited for garages, as they operate better in cool temperatures and are more energy efficient than T12s.

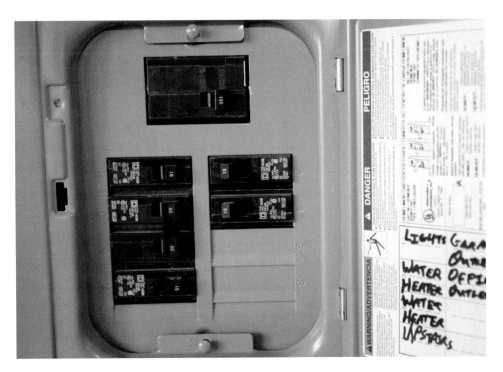

Your typical fuse box. Notice how quickly 100-amp service fills up when you have one big draw (in this case, a boiler for an in-floor heating system).

Track lighting provides the directional light on this window seat in an above-garage space (see pages 82–83). If you are building an over-the-top garage, you can use this technique to light portions of the garage.

If your garage is going to be at 50 degrees or less, get fixtures equipped with electronic (rather than electromagnetic) ballasts, as they are rated to work at 0 degrees or lower. And if you regularly see temperatures below zero, heat your garage. Better yet, move.

For places in which you need to see colors clearly, the color-rendering index (CRI) of the light bulbs you choose is significant. You'll want a CRI of 85 or more for painting, wood finishing, or any other activity that requires accurate lighting. Finding these ratings on product packaging can be tricky—your best bet is to look for them on the manufacturer's Web site or in their product catalog.

Recessed lighting is actually not that expensive, and it looks terrific. It is a bit of overkill for a garage, but maybe that's your goal. Use the cans that hold the larger R40

bulbs, as you can get these in 50- to 120-watt outputs. Plus, they are cheaper than the smaller cans. In a house, you'd want a can every 4 feet or so, but that is more than you need in a garage—every 6 feet is plenty, and you can even stretch it out to 8 feet and be fine. Again, check out the GE Web site to do your calculations.

Consider two of the popular energy-efficient bulbs on the market for your garage. Compact fluorescent lights (CFLs) are four times more efficient than garden-variety incandescent light bulbs and can last up to 10 times longer. They are not ideal for a garage, however, because they aren't great for lots of switching on and off (as most people do in their garage). Also, they lose power at lower temperatures, which is an issue if your garage is unheated and you live in a cooler climate.

 Light-emitting diode (LED) bulbs are roughly 133 times longer-lasting than incandescent bulbs and use less than 20 percent of the energy. These are not great for overhead use, as

Install an Outlet

Supplies: Outlet box, outlet cover, wire nuts
Tools: Phillips screwdriver
Time: 10 minutes
Tab: $10

Wiring is one of those things that is very simple to do but requires your full attention. Screw it up, and the consequences are anywhere from shocking to dire.

Every now and again, you need to replace an outlet (especially if you happen to burn one out by overloading the breaker).

It's simple, cheap, and takes about 10 minutes of your time. Just pay attention, OK?

First, turn off the breaker switch so there's no power going to your box. Plug in a light to make sure that the power is really cut off before you start! Remove the old switch plate with the single screw in the center.

Remove the two screws holding the outlet in place.

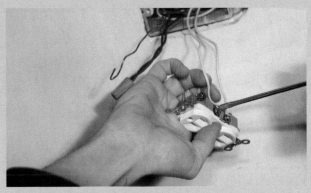

Pull off the ground wire.

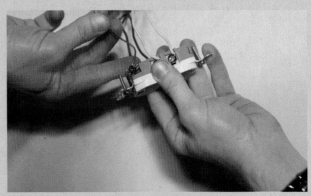

Remove the wires from the left and right of the outlet.

Notice the overhead fluorescent lighting in this garage bay. These are spaced fairly tightly to give good light and even more tightly in the back part of the room where most of the fine detail work takes place.

the light they emit tends to be directional rather than radiant (though a few manufacturers are creating LED bulbs that replace fluorescent tubes).

LED bulbs are, however, excellent (if expensive) choices for lighting work areas, as the light is bright and directional and they use very little energy. As a bonus, they are more rugged than traditional light bulbs or CFL bulbs. In 2007, prices for a simple LED bulb were as high as $40. That should change in the coming years, and LED bulbs will become economical enough to be practical choices.

PLUMBING

Running water, gas lines, and sewer service are all useful additions to a garage. These are another consideration that typically don't add a lot of cost when you are building, as you can run the lines in the same trench that is dug to tap into your home's electrical service.

Bear in mind that you may require more involved permits and inspections if you add sewer and water service

to your garage. Check with city hall about the local building codes.

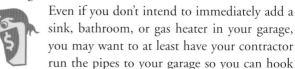 Even if you don't intend to immediately add a sink, bathroom, or gas heater in your garage, you may want to at least have your contractor run the pipes to your garage so you can hook that up further down the road. It costs relatively little to do this when you build. If you decide to do these things at a later date, the costs are much higher and may require intensive "surgery" to your garage and yard.

Floor Drains

The plumbing that you will find most useful in a garage is also the most basic: a floor drain. This is a great feature, as it allows you to wash the floor or even wash your vehicles inside the garage. Be very careful, though, about what you wash down the drain. Pouring oil, gasoline, or other chemicals will do serious damage to the environment.

Check your local ordinances. Some places allow you to simply create a small drain field under the garage, while others require that the drain taps into the sewer system.

The Garage Sink

Running water is a great thing to have in a garage, and the

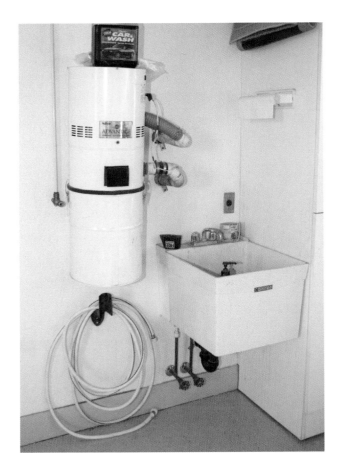

A laundry or utility sink is ideal for the garage. You can find complete kits for less than $100 at home improvement stores. This garage is also equipped with air lines running along the perimeter of the shop area, which allow the owner to hook up a large compressor at one end and have pressurized air sockets available to power tools or air up tires. Note the central vacuum system as well.

Heaven on Earth (aka the Garage Restroom)

If you took the trouble to run sewer and water service to your garage, it might make sense to go all out and put in a restroom. Keep in mind, however, that you will have significant permit and inspection considerations to deal with if you install a bathroom. Make sure all the work you do is inspected, as you'll find that some states require your realtor to check whether or not you had recent renovations done with the proper inspections.

A small restroom is a great addition to your garage, but if you live in a cool climate, it also means the garage needs to be heated. Also, you'll need to allow room to frame the room's walls and put in a toilet and sink. And if you want to mount a toilet on the first floor, remember to make plumbing accommodations when the concrete is poured.

 Composting toilets are an option if you didn't run water and sewer service out to the garage. These are fairly slick units that will turn your waste into compost and don't require plumbing. They cost $1,200 and up, but that may be cheaper than running sewage pipes.

 Mr. Cheapskate, you can build yourself a self-composting unit with a 55-gallon drum and plans found on the Web. Unless you happen to be a rocket scientist who can get every detail of the plan right, I'm never going to use it, and I'd bet most of your friends will feel the same way. But knock yourself out.

continued on page 84

This garage sink is hardly pretty, but it sees daily use by the boys in the Texican Chop Shop in San Angelo, Texas. This kind of sink is ideal to wash out air filters, paint brushes, or whatever other nasty shop jobs you need done.

easiest way to do that is with a sink. A big laundry sink is ideal; if you have a floor drain, you can run a hose off the sink's faucet and wash your toys in the garage, or simply wash down the floor.

The sink also can be used to wash parts, air filters, and your grease-covered carcass. If you like a little adventure in your marital life, wash out a dirty air filter in the kitchen sink and see how your spouse reacts to the foul-smelling grease pit that results. If you prefer a more peaceful coexistence at home, install a garage sink and clean your air filters out there.

If you're dealing with an existing garage that has no water lines, a plumber can tap into your system. If you are building, at the very least consider running the lines in the walls so you can hook them up later, as this becomes more complex (not to mention expensive) once walls are covered in sheetrock.

Save Money on Utilities

What You'll Need: Common sense
Time: 2–20 minutes
Tab: Cheap

This is really another part of being green, as the less power you use the more left-footed red parableebs you'll save in Bora Bora. I know you don't really care about the red-footed parableeb. But you probably are a cheapskate, right? Well, read on—these tips will save you the agony of writing big checks to your local power company. And that's something we can all get behind!

- Use fans instead of air conditioning to cool the garage. A big fan and an open garage door can cool your garage amazingly quickly. When the evening gets cool, open that big garage door and blow the hot air out the front and let the cool air come in. If your garage is insulated, it will retain the cool air for at least part of the next day.

- Install a ceiling fan in your garage. This will move the air around and keep it cool much more efficiently than air conditioning.

- Turn off the lights when you aren't in the garage. Plug all of your electrical appliances (rechargeable-battery power station, grinder, etc.) into power strips that you can turn off when you are out. All electrical appliances use a little bit of power even when they are turned off—plugging them into a power strip and turning it off will save you a few bucks.

- Install energy-efficient lighting. See the section on lighting for details on this.

- When you wash your car or motorcycle, use a big bucket of soapy water and turn the hose off while you are washing. When you have washed the entire car, rinse it off with the hose as quickly as possible. Oh, and if your faucet leaks, fix it!

- If you heat your garage, use a programmable thermostat, and set it to heat the garage only when you are out there. And insulate your garage access door so you aren't blowing heat up into that unheated second floor or storage truss space.

- Plant trees that will shade your garage.

- Use solar heat to your advantage. On cold days, open the blinds and let the sun warm your space. On hot days, close the blinds when the sun is shining in.

- Install dimmer switches and motion sensors. Dimmed light bulbs last up to 20 times longer and motion sensors turn on lights only when you need them.

- Install motion sensor–triggered outdoor lighting.

- Install a floor-mounted garage door threshold seal, which will better seal your garage from the elements.

- If you use an in-floor heater with an external tank water heater, insulate the water heater tank.

- If you have a television in the garage, switch it off and turn on the radio if you are listening to a sporting event. The TV is one of the major power-users in any household, so unless you are watching it, turn it off.

- Replace all nonessential lighting with lower-wattage bulbs. You will need good light above work areas, but you don't need all that much light to find your way out of your car and into the house, for example. Use 40-watt bulbs in the overheads rather than 100-watt bulbs.

- Insulate heated and air-conditioned spaces. You can add a layer of batting above these spaces and save yourself some heating costs if you heat the garage all winter long or even on a semiregular basis.

- If you heat the garage, wear a heavy sweatshirt while you're working out there. No need to heat that space to 70 degrees, especially if you're moving around a lot.

- Use Great Stuff brand foam or other spray foam to seal the spaces around windows and doors. You'll need to do this before sheetrocking and trimming the doors and windows. And remember: if sealing around doors, buy the door formula; if sealing around windows, use the window formula. Many a door frame has been pushed out of square by the denser window foam.

Air conditioning is nice in a garage, but a big fan will do the job on all but the hottest days. Simple things like this will save you money and are good for the environment as well. A win-win.

- Get a separate water meter for your hoses. In most parts of the country, you pay for sewer usage based on your water meter reading. Why pay for the sewer when the water was used to water the lawn or wash your chopper?

- Clean the coils on the back of your garage fridge. Refrigerators are one of the biggest consumers of power in the house or garage. Don't waste a bunch of money keeping your beer cold (not to say that isn't important!).

- Find out if your utility company offers free energy audits. With this service, they will come out, inspect your property, and make suggestions on how to save some money on your utility bills.

This art studio above a garage uses a great combination of natural light, overhead light, and warm lights reflected off the walls to blend ambience with functional light. Note the pegboard covering over the forced-air furnace in the back corner, which cleans up the look and provides a place to hang tools and supplies.

Garage plumbing can also be used to create a full kitchen, a great addition if your garage is a place to entertain.

continued from page 79

HEATING

If you want to use your garage on a regular basis, regulating the temperature may be a priority. In the northern states and Canada, a heated garage makes the winter months a bit easier, and as a bonus your car will be warm even when it's below zero outside.

You have an assortment of options available for heat. If your garage is already built but heat-free, you can use a freestanding heater. The larger electrical units kick out plenty of heat and are fairly safe. The freestanding gas and propane units are a bit more risky due to the fact that they use flames (not good in any space where you store your gas cans) and produce fumes. Use them with caution.

If you want a safer, more efficient solution, you can hang a natural gas heater from the ceiling or affix it to the wall. These are relatively cheap, costing between $200 and $600, and most of the modern units vent simply and produce plenty of heat.

Despite the manufacturers' claims that venting will eliminate all odors from your space, these gas heaters do produce a smell. In fact, on some of the lower-end, between-the-stud models, the smell is quite strong.

With gas prices on the rise, ceiling-mounted electrical heaters have become a reasonable alternative. These units are priced comparably to gas units and have the advantage of no emissions. Plus, they use your electrical system, so you don't have to deal with the expense and hassle of having a gas line run to your garage. Remember to consider a heater when you're planning your wiring (see previous).

 If you are a cheapskate, the hot tip is to find an old home furnace and hook it up properly. These kick out lots of heat, vent wonderfully if installed to spec, and can be found for next to nothing if you are willing to scrounge around. These re-used units can be perfect if you only spend a few weekends a year out in the garage, as you can turn them on only when you want to heat it.

If you spend significant time in your garage, however, consider in-floor radiant heat. These systems heat the concrete slab with fluid that is circulated through reinforced plastic tubing. Of course, you'll need to put the tubing down before the slab is poured and then install some kind of water heater to warm the fluid, along with a valve system and thermostat to regulate the temperature.

 Cheapskates, laying out the tubing for your in-floor heating system before the concrete is poured is a fairly easy job. Only do this if you can be very, very careful not to nick the hose. A cut in the hose will make your entire system leak and not function properly and will require the concrete to be torn up so the nick can be patched. And don't ask me why I know this—the person responsible for the Tubing Fiasco is considered He Who Shall Not Be Named in my household.

Radiant in-floor heating is efficient, as the slab will hold the heat (provided your concrete guy insulates it properly). Plus, there are no drafts from forced-air heat and a warm floor underneath you as you work. I've heard stories of guys with in-floor heat who have trouble working underneath their cars. The floor is so warm and comfortable that they fall asleep every time they lie down on it to work on the car!

The primary heat source is simply a water heater, but this needs to be selected carefully. A storage water heater will do the job but may not meet code and has the disadvantage of heating the water in the tank whether or not you need heat in the floor. Storage water heaters, on the other hand, can become overloaded by the demands of the system.

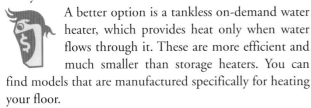 A better option is a tankless on-demand water heater, which provides heat only when water flows through it. These are more efficient and much smaller than storage heaters. You can find models that are manufactured specifically for heating your floor.

Tankless and storage-tank water heaters are available in both natural gas and electric models. Electrics were more economical to operate when this book was written. Plus, they eliminate the additional expense of stringing gas lines into your garage. I also suggest you avoid having the small pilot flame of a gas heater going in your garage if you intend to store fuel or other combustibles in there.

Electric on-demand tankless water heaters are efficient and were commonly available when this book went to press. You can also consider heat-pump, solar, and indirect water heaters.

Whatever you use, I highly recommend working with an experienced shop that specializes in the heat source of your choice. The electrical needs and hookup of these units can be complex, and using an experienced professional will make the installation less painful.

COOLING

Fans are the simplest means of cooling your garage, and a big one cranking away with the door or windows open will cool the space down efficiently. If you can do this at night when the air is cool, a well-insulated garage will stay temperate most of the time.

Ceiling fans are another option. These are great for offices, game rooms, and other living spaces. They will keep the air moving cheaply and efficiently.

Air conditioning is another nice feature in a garage and can be quite cheap as well. Air conditioners are rated by their BTU (British thermal units) per hour output. You

In-floor heat requires a water heater, valve system, control box, and an air tank to keep the lines from getting air-locked. The Hydro-Shark is the water heater used here. It provides 11 1/2 kilowatts of heating power (more than twice that of a typical home water heater). The valve system is controlled by the green box, which is hooked to a thermostat in each of the heating zones. Tankless heaters are more powerful than typical residential water heaters and much more efficient.

can figure out your needs with several online calculators that input the size of the room, sun exposure, and how important the cooling is to you.

If you have double-hung windows in your garage, simply install a window-mounted unit. Another solution is to install a wall-mounted unit, which can be purchased for $100 to $400. When building a new garage, have your contractor frame a small unit into the garage wall. Don't forget to have your electrician put an outlet near the air conditioner mount as well.

 Swamp coolers are another option for cooling your garage. A swamp cooler is simply a fan that blows outside air past wet pads and into the house. The evaporation of the water cools the air by about 20 degrees. You can purchase these commercially. A true cheapskate can build their own—again, plans are readily available online.

If you are going over the top with your garage, install central heating and air conditioning. This is most practical with attached garages when you can tap into your home system.

The garage bathroom is another useful plumbing addition. If you are building a new structure, consider running water and sewer lines to the garage so you can add a sink or bathroom down the road.

Install an Autocloser

Supplies: Autocloser kit
Tools: 3/8-inch-drive ratchet and deep-well sockets, Combination wrench, Phillips screwdriver, wire stripper
Time: 30 minutes
Tab: $49.95

Leaving the garage door open is one of the easiest ways to invite a robbery, particularly for those of us whose garages are stuffed with motorcycles, hot rods, sports cars, or other eye-catching (and easy-to-steal) vehicles.

This kind of theft is common, and law enforcement Web sites everywhere warn you to close your garage door anytime you are not in the garage.

Remote-control garage doors can easily be left open, if unintentionally. A stray leaf can blow in and trigger the sensor at the bottom of the door and cause it to reopen, or you can simply forget to close the door. A garage door that's open all day is simply an invitation for robbery!

Xceltronix has developed a simple solution: a little device called the Autocloser that automatically closes your door after it has been open for a preset amount of time. The device ties in to your existing garage door closer with a fairly simple installation, while still allowing your remote and the emergency trip to work as they always have.

Once it's installed, you can set the time limit at 5, 10, 15, or 20 minutes. After your set period of time, the Autocloser will beep several times, close the door partially, and then close it fully. The kit includes a disable switch; press this, and the garage door will stay open as long as you like (if, for example, you are working in the garage on a nice day and want to leave the door open).

Close the door, and the Autocloser engages again for the next time you open the door. It's simple and cheap and will ensure that your garage door is closed when you intend it to be closed.

Left: *Bolt this plastic reflector to your garage door–opening mechanism arm. You should be able to use the existing bolt to fasten the plastic reflector to the arm.*

Right: *The Autocloser fastens to the bottom of your garage door opener with Velcro strips. Fasten these onto the Autocloser.*

87

Line up the Autocloser with the reflector mounted to your garage door opener arm. The sensor should point toward the reflector. Note that the Velcro strips hold the unit on the garage door opener quite securely.

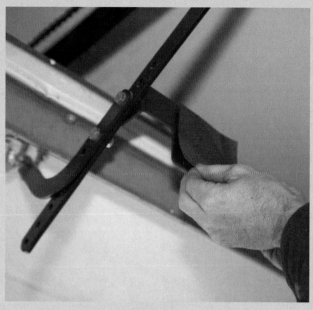

The reflector gets covered with this adhesive piece of reflective paper. Once the paper is on, switch the Autocloser to "test" and plug it in. If the reflector and the sensor are properly aligned, the Autocloser will sound a continuous tone.

Strip several sets of jumper wires. Run these from your garage door closer to the Autocloser.

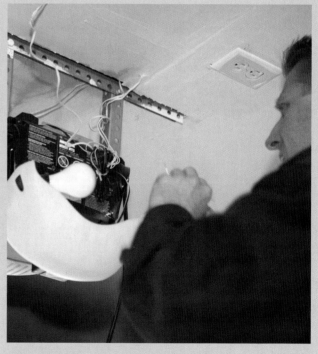

Connect the jumper wire to your garage door opener. In this case, the wires simply slipped into the garage door closer wire sockets in the LiftMaster garage door opener. The directions for the Autocloser include detailed instructions about how to connect to your garage door opener.

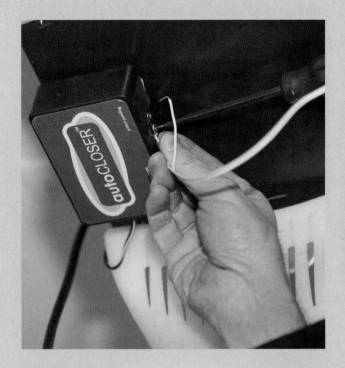

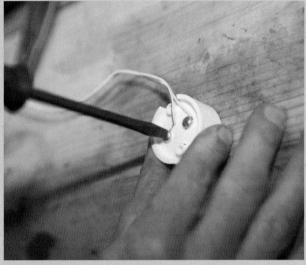

Left: *Connect the other end of the jumper from your garage door opener to the "NO" terminals on the Autocloser.* **Above:** *The "disable" button has to be hooked up to the Autocloser using a long wire.*

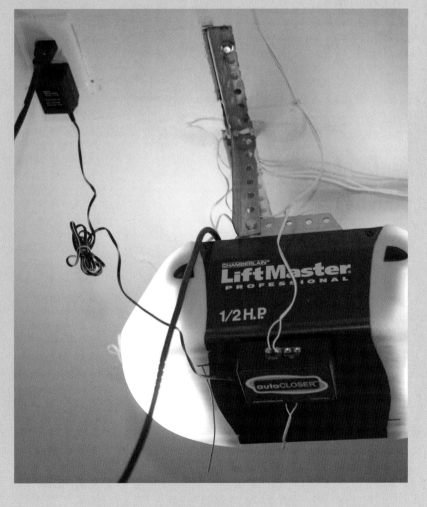

Above: *Mount the disable button on the wall near your control for your garage door opener.*

Right: *String the wire from the disable button across the wall and up to the Autocloser. Connect those wires as directed, and you are ready to go. You can use the unit right out of the box if you want a 5-minute delay before the garage door automatically closes. If you would prefer a 10-, 15-, or 20-minute delay, you can program it in fairly simply.*

CHAPTER 4
WORKSPACES

A garage can be a haven, a place to go when you need to escape into the world of torque wrenches, turbochargers, and tuning. Set up your space correctly, and those hours will be a joy.

The key is to put some planning into making the space useful and logically laid out. For starters, what do you plan to do in your garage? That will determine your space needs and layout.

If you plan to do a lot of different things in your space, consider setting up your garage to be flexible by using rolling tool carts, benches, and stands. This is particularly useful for large garage floors with lots of vehicles inside. You can move your work area to the machine you are working on rather than having to move the car, truck, or motorcycle around the shop.

If you do build fixed workspaces, go back to the floor plan you drew up while designing the general structure. Make a list of all the equipment you want to incorporate into the garage, and then draw them into the floor plan. Either leave space to move around in the garage or assume that you are going to move one or more of your vehicles out of the space before beginning your work.

A station for your grinder is always useful, but be sure to locate it far away from any flammable materials. You also may want to consider a small space for a drill press and another for a vise and an air compressor.

Some other things to consider adding to the drawing are a parts-cleaning station and a place for sandblasting equipment (ideal for restorers). If you fancy yourself a home fabricator (and who doesn't), consider setting aside some space for a welding station and/or a lathe and maybe even other, more exotic machining and fabricating tools.

Another useful addition is a rolling chair and a desk. This gives you a place to sit down and do fine work such as rebuilding carburetors. This is also a great place to put your laptop computer if you use one or to sit and draw plans for your next hot rod or custom motorcycle. Make sure such a space has the right lighting.

Get measurements, draw carefully, and don't be afraid to juggle things around a bit on paper. You'll also naturally move the layout around as time passes and you work on it. As with the design of the structure, a well thought-out workspace will give you better odds that your garage will meet your work needs.

This well-designed workspace is in a motorcycle customization shop. The metal walls are an economical way to give the space a flashy, industrial look.

WORKBENCHES

If you belong to the gearhead race, a workbench is essential. This will be your center of operations, the place where carburetors are cleaned, bent stuff is hammered straight, and (if, like me, you enjoy hosting parties in your garage) bean dip gets spilled.

Your choices here are pretty extensive. You can spend a whole bunch of money on a top-of-the-line commercial tool bench with impenetrable poly coatings or galvanized sheet-metal surfaces, or you can spend not very much and build your own.

You want to have a solid bench capable of bearing several hundred pounds. When the time comes to put a motorcycle engine (or rear end) on the bench and work on it, you'll be set.

Place the bench in a well-lit area that is a bit off the traffic pattern and in close proximity to where you'll be doing the work. Allow for some space in front of the bench for the project you enjoy working on. Motorcycle people don't need a large space nearby, while the monster truck set will need a larger workspace near the bench.

Also, avoid putting the bench close to the door, as you'll tend to use it as a storage space.

Above: In this Seattle warehouse, the workspace is tucked into a corner, and cars can be wheeled into it. Shelves and simple countertops ring the area, providing plenty of bench space for projects.

Opposite: Need to put your bike up in the air and move it around? You can build a cart like this one for just a few bucks.

The Bargain Bench

At the most basic level, you can draw up a simple plan, go down to your local home improvement store, and buy a pile of 2x4s and nail a bench together. You can accomplish this with less than $20 (you can find plans for a $20 bench at http://www.hammerzone.com/archives/workshop/bench/below20.html).

If you do one of these quick and dirty home builds, include a heavy-duty top in your design. Two-inch pine works well. If you can find arrow-straight 2x12s, two of them make a solid, level top. One-inch plywood is another good choice to provide a stout, sturdy work surface.

If you are made of money, kitchen countertops make great workbench tops. Better yet, go down to your local retailer to see if they have some scrap in the back. You just

Above: *A bookshelf is a great addition to your workspace.*

Opposite top: *This workspace packs in a sandblaster and benches. When you are laying out your workspace, get measurements of the equipment you want to use so you can design it to make the machinery easily accessible.*

Opposite bottom: *A desk area to keep paperwork can be created in a larger space by building a simple wall.*

might find something long enough that the storekeeper is looking to unload for cheap.

The surface of your workbench should be from 24 to 36 inches wide. Any deeper, and you won't be able to reach the back easily; go any narrower, and you won't have enough space to work.

A good workbench should be 30 to 36 inches tall. Taller benches should be above elbow height, while benches designed for working on engines or other heavy equipment should be just below your elbows.

Length is a matter of taste and need. If you rarely use your bench and don't plan to install a vise or other bench-mounted equipment, an 8-foot bench is adequate.

But who wants adequate? If your space permits it, go for 12 feet or longer.

Purchasing Workbenches

If money is no object, you can find some incredible workbenches out there. Most come in packages that include matching cabinets, so you can outfit and color-coordinate your garage.

You can find these packages made out of aluminum, stainless steel, and galvanized sheet metal. The resources section in the back of this book includes a number of attractive choices to "pimp" your garage.

Rolling Workbenches

A portable workspace is a great addition to nearly any garage. When working on cars, motorcycles, tractors, or even bicycles, a portable place to rest tools, parts, and whatever else you need for the job is extremely useful.

You can build a portable wooden bench fairly simply. Find a plan for a small bench that includes casters or modify an existing plan to include casters.

You can also purchase metal and plastic rolling benches at your local home improvement store.

Whether you build or buy, look for a bench that is sturdy and includes a lip around the edge so that parts don't roll off and onto the floor (or down the floor drain—don't ask how I know about that one).

continued on page 100

Build a Simple Workbench

Supplies: *Note that all lumber is construction-grade pine.* 4 8-foot 2x4s, 2 8-foot 4x4s, 2 10-foot 2x6s, 1 6-foot 2x6, 100 2 1/2–inch wood screws, 16 3 1/2-inch-long 5/16-inch lag screws or 16 5-inch-long 5/16-inch lag bolts, 4x8 sheet of 1/2-inch plywood

Tools: Cordless drill, 1/4-inch drill bit, 5/16-inch wood bit, Chuck and Phillips bit, circular saw, square, pencil, measuring tape, ratchet and deep-well socket, rubber mallet

Time: 2–3 hours

Tab: $80–$100

Building a workbench is a genuine pleasure. It goes together easily, doesn't cost a lot of money, and is fairly forgiving of the inevitable small mistakes made by novice carpenters.

This example is an extremely sturdy workbench that can be built in an afternoon. The 4x4 posts make it as solid as a rock. The dimensions for our bench were dictated by the fact that it is being used in my friend's basement. The bench is 42 inches high, 60 inches long, and 27 1/2 inches deep.

The 42-inch height is great for more dexterous work like rebuilding carburetors, but maybe a little high if you intend to do a lot of hammering. The 60-inch length is fine. If space permits, I suggest making it 6 or 8 feet long, just for the convenience of using standard-sized lumber.

The depth is that of five 2x6s and is adequate for most gearhead jobs. If you work on a lot of bulky parts, you might want to add another 2x6 or two and make it 33 or 38 1/2 inches deep. You can also add one more 2x6 and turn the back one up on end, which gives you a little backstop on the bench.

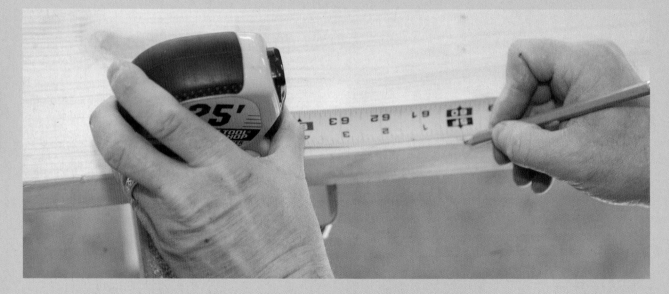

Above: *Start by cutting all your pieces to size. See the cut list below to build a bench of the same dimensions as we did. You can easily modify the dimensions to suit your tastes.*

Top of bench	60-inch 2x6s (5)
Legs	40 1/2–inch 4x4s (4)
Support Box Sides	54-inch 2x4s (4)
Support Box Ends	20 1/2-inch 2x4s (4)

Right: *Large diamond grinders can be rented at most tool rental places. This one is the WerkMaster Octi-Disc, which uses eight floating discs to grind the floor.*

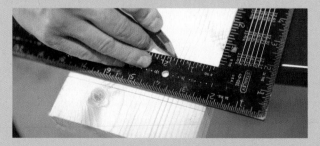

Mark your cut with a square. If you are cutting with a circular saw, make a second mark to use as a guide for the saw's fence.

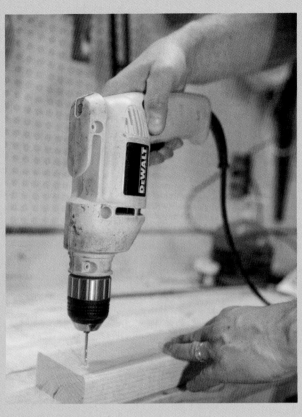

Above: The second line next to the cut gives you a visual guide to keep the fence parallel to the line. A compound miter saw will make perfectly square cuts, but a circular saw is adequate for this job.

Right: The first pieces we built were the top and bottom support boxes. Predrill the 2x4s so that the wood screws don't split the wood.

Left: Lay the pieces on a square surface and fasten them with wood screws. We screwed it together loosely, with the screws just barely tightened, checked that everything was square, and then tightened the corners.

Right: Here's the completed support box. Build two of these.

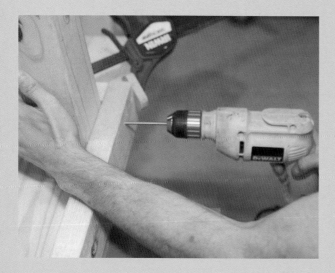

Above: *Lay out one of the support boxes on a square surface (we used a sheet of pine board on two sawhorses) and put the four posts in the corners. Clamp them tightly into the corners as shown and predrill the holes for your lag screws or bolts with a 5/16-inch drill bit.*

Right: *Lag bolts will need to be hammered through and then fastened with nuts and washers.*

Left: *Flip the bench onto its legs and fasten the lower support box. We positioned it about 4 inches off the ground.*

Right: *By covering the bottom support box in sheeting, you create a nice lower shelf and add a little stability. We found a pine board made of glued strips that was nearly exactly the right size and was priced only slightly more than a sheet of 1/2-inch plywood. Either works fine—the glued pine is just a bit stouter and better-looking. Cut the board to length.*

WORKSPACES

Carefully measure the distance between the legs, then transfer the measurement to your bottom board. Make the bottom board about 1/8 inch narrower than the opening—you'll need a little bit of wiggle room to slide the board in place.

Once the board is cut to length, notches need to be cut out so it will slide in between the legs. We used a handsaw, which allows for a cleaner cut in the corners.

Tap the board into place with a rubber mallet and fasten it to the frame with wood screws.

Screw the top boards onto the frame, and you have a finished workbench. The top can be glued together to make it a bit smoother and more rugged, which was done in this case, after the bench was carried down into the basement.

continued from page 95

A Better Home-Built Bench

Cheap benches are fine for the practical-minded, but if you were that type, you probably wouldn't have bought a book about your garage. One of the great things about the increased interest in DIY these days is that you can find some terrific plans for high-quality home-built furniture.

So here's a better option for the DIY types who want a bench that is both functional and attractive: http://www.plansnow.com/wkbmechanic.html.

Folding Workbenches

Another option for the portable workspace is a folding bench. These are pretty slick if you have a small garage or don't use your bench all that often. They don't tend to be as sturdy as the permanent variety, but they often are cheap.

LIGHTING YOUR BENCH

Once the bench is built, string up some good light. A nice mix is an overhead light above the space with a retractable light to provide extra illumination when you need it.

Putting the bench under a garage window will provide some natural light during the day and is particularly nice if you spend a lot of time working there. Just bear in mind

The fellas at the Texican Chop Shop in San Angelo, Texas, use this rolling tool chest as a workspace.

that you will want to include shutters so you can prevent prying eyes from figuring out that your garage houses a collection of racing Porsches (or something else expensive and easy to steal).

COMPUTERIZING YOUR BENCH

 Are you using your computer in the garage? More and more people are, whether to adjust tunable ignition systems or to do a Google search to find out how to change the light bulb in a Cagiva motorcycle. You can order racks with swinging arms to hang your laptop off the edge of the bench, or you can just build the bench a little wider.

POWERING YOUR BENCH

You are going to want plenty of outlets on the workbench (see Chapter Three for more about this). On the actual bench, consider adding switch boxes so you can turn on your lights, grinder, air compressor, or even the radio.

Drop-down lights are ideal for workbenches, as they put good light right on top of your project. If you mount

100

This rolling tool chest features a roll-down screen that can be locked when you are away from your tools.

shelves above the workbench, which is a good way to use that space effectively, you can mount the lights under the shelves as well.

ADDING THE TOOLS YOU NEED

Once you have your workbench sorted out, you'll want to have the tools you use regularly out in the open. Position your toolboxes so they are easy to reach when you are at your bench or work area. An interesting alternative to a workbench is to use a rolling tool chest as one of your work surfaces. These tools chests are mounted on wheels and have flat tops that give you another workspace that can be rolled around and used for projects elsewhere in the garage.

Cover the wall behind the bench in pegboard, and you can hang the tools you use most often there (see Chapter Five for more on the ins and outs of pegboard).

You can also suspend tools from a 2x4 beam that runs over the top of the workbench. This is a great place to put air tools, drills, and other relatively light power tools, and it allows you to reach up and grab tools that you use often.

This workbench can be built from plans supplied by August Home Publishing. Building this bench requires solid woodworking skills, unlike the simpler bench kits you can find at your home improvement store. August Home Publishing

Above: *Plastic rolling carts are fairly cheap, and the tray at the top is useful for keeping parts organized while you work.*

Opposite: *Tool carts work well as portable workspaces that can be rolled to your project.*

Right: *A simple wooden stool makes the front of this garage near Portland, Washington, one of the owner's favorite places to work on his collection of vintage Farmall tractors.*

Light Your Workbench

Supplies: New lights
Tools: Cordless drill, 1/4-inch drill bit, Chuck and Phillips bit, pencil, measuring tape
Time: 20 minutes and up
Tab: $10–$50

Ample light over your workbench is a must, and mounting lights is a simple project anyone can do.

In this case, the lights were attached to an overhead shelf unit. You can also hang them from the ceiling by lengths of chain, another effective way to ensure the light is close to the bench surface. You overly anal sorts can also wire switches so that you can turn on the lights with a switch at bench level. Personally, I don't mind reaching up to switch the light on, but you have to admire the effort put in by those switch-on-the-bench sorts.

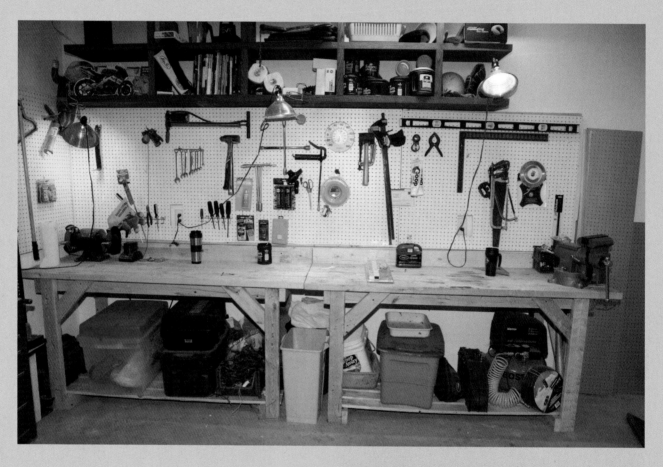

Above: *This bench was in the shadows, no thanks to an overhead shelf unit. The quick fix was these cheapo clamp-on lights. They are great to bring in as added light but inadequate for a bench. They move around, fall down every now and again, and look terrible. It was time for an upgrade.*

Right: *You can find a variety of good lights down at your home improvement store. Mounting them is a piece of cake. Flip the light over and mark where to put the screws into your shelf.*

Measure your marks to make sure they are even.

Drill pilot holes for the wood screws.

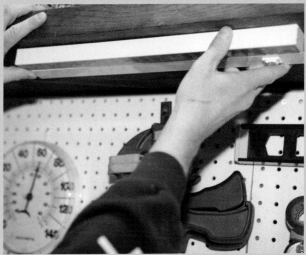

Left: *Drive the screws in. Leave the heads about 3/16 inch above the surface so that the light can slide on.*

Above: *Slide the light unit in place and plug it in. Wasn't that easy?*

CHAPTER 5
STORAGE OPTIONS

The garage is a great place to store things—which typically leads to a complete disaster. Want to do better? If you are a cheapskate (like me) and at best modestly talented at building things (also like me), the garage is a great place to make the most of your questionable carpentry skills.

Building shelving and other simple storage places in the garage is something well within the capabilities of all but the most fumble-fingered. The best part? If it looks a little less-than-show quality, who cares? It's your garage!

For those of you concerned with appearance, you can explain away the imperfections that result from a beginner's attempt at carpentry as *wabi-sabi*, a Japanese concept that refers to finding beauty in imperfection.

Garage storage falls into four key categories: wall storage, shelving, cabinets, and overhead storage. Well, make that five—any good garage has to have a place for beer (or cold beverage of your choice)!

If you've got deep pockets, well, all you have to do is call up one of those garage storage places and have someone come out and hang fancy cabinets, wall coverings, and storage bins. Maybe you can even hire the neighbor kid to put everything on the wall for you so you don't have to lift a finger. This will probably cost you $10,000 or so, but what do you care? You're made of money.

Cheapskates, you are going to want to be strategic about this part of finishing your garage. The first question is where to put things, right?

Well, you want to have things you use a lot readily at hand. Group tools around your workbench, and if you are an avid cyclist, for example, have the bicycle and accessories easy to access.

Things that you use less often are good candidates for shelves and ceiling-mounted storage. If you have a ton of camping gear, for example, but only go once or twice a year, get that stuff up and out of your way.

Four-post stands allow you to maximize space if your garage has a high enough ceiling. This one uses hand cranks to lift the cars. These types of simple lifts can be used to work underneath your vehicles and for storage purposes. Be sure to put some kind of liner or catch pan under older cars or anything that might leak—a tiny drip of coolant can damage the paint job of the car below.

1985 DP 935

Cabinets provide useful storage space but also clean up the look of your garage. SwissTrax

WALL STORAGE

If you have open stud walls, you can fill in that space and store things fairly easily. Build simple shelves by nailing 2x4 crosspieces between the studs, and hang all kinds of things off nails pounded into the studs.

More sophisticated sorts can pound two nails side by side into the stud, with just enough space in between to hang the item in question.

You can also string a bungee cord across some open studs to store long items like skis, rakes, and pitchforks. Simply slide the item behind the bungee cord, and it's tucked away, out of harm.

Hooks can be screwed into your studs as well. You can find a pack of rubber-coated ones down at your local home improvement store for about $10. Screw one or two into the rafters and hang a bicycle upside down, freeing up some floor space in the process.

These storage solutions are all simple, cheap, and effective. But put just a little bit of forethought into the process, or you'll end up with junk hanging all over your garage in a completely random pattern and will never, ever be able to find anything except what you don't need.

Pegboard

Honestly, the whole nail-in-the-stud setup is pretty low rent and inflexible. The classic way to store tools is to tack a sheet of pegboard above your workbench and hang up the tools you use on a regular basis. It's cheap, effective, and easy (see Chapter Four). This also frees up some space in your toolbox.

The cheapest pegboard can be purchased at your local home improvement store and is pressed board with 9/32-inch-diameter holes spaced an inch apart. Expect to pay less than $20 for a 4x8-foot sheet. You can find it in dark tan, white, and silver.

One note: When you buy pegs to hang your tools, find the larger-diameter pegs. Half the time, the smaller-diameter variety will pull out when you take the tool off the wall and drive you nuts in the process. You can also purchase pegboard hooks with little screws that lock them to the board to prevent this.

Other options are polypropylene and stainless-steel pegboard. The poly units cost about $50 for a 4x8 sheet, while the steel sheets run $200 and up for 4x8 feet of coverage. The steel is typically sold in smaller sheets, as it is much more economical to ship. The steel sheets come with round holes sized traditionally or with larger square holes. The square-holed variety is designed to hold heavier tools, and a 24x24-inch sheet is typically rated to hold 250 to 400 pounds of tools.

One warning: Spending hours organizing tools on your pegboard is a sign that you are officially a garage freak. Accept it and move on. If you draw outlines around them so you know which tool goes where (and are not working with tools professionally), you have a problem. Get help.

Slat-Wall Systems

For those of you swanky folk with sheetrocked walls, you have lots of options. Let's start at the low-cost end of things: you too can hang pegboard using furring strips.

Slat wall is another effective storage option. These come in sheets, and accessories can be purchased that allow you to hang nearly anything on the wall. Washingtonspaces.com

A number of companies offer wall storage options that will help you organize things by mounting slat-wall systems and then clipping in their accessories. These look terrific and are sturdy enough to hang heavy tools on. You've seen this stuff before—it's quite popular with retail outlets.

The best option for this, in my opinion, is to buy unpainted slat wall in 4x8 sheets. I found it for as little as $30 per panel. The retailer I used had baskets, hooks, and shelving as well. The cost for a system like this to cover an 8x16-foot wall, including shipping, was about $200. That's pretty reasonable and provides a good-looking way to hang just about anything.

All kinds of garage-oriented businesses provide slat-wall systems designed specifically for the garage. This material is better-looking and more expensive than the more unfinished stuff described above. Flashy stainless-steel slat wall and pegboard sheeting runs about $200 per 4x8 sheet, and accessories are also expensive. I priced out covering an 8x16 wall, including accessories, and it came out to about $800.

continued on page 114

Install a Pegboard Wall Hanger

Supplies: 1x2-inch pine boards (enough to edge entire project), 1x4-inch pine boards (for vertical pieces used to connect two sheets), 2 1/2–inch wood screws, 1 1/2–inch wood screws, pegboard sheets, pegboard hooks

Tools: Cordless drill, Chuck and drill bits, screwdriver bits, level, hammer, jigsaw, tape measure, square, pencil, chalk line

Time: 1–2 hours (depending on size of area covered)

Tab: $40–$100 (depending on area covered)
Pegboard is one of the most versatile ways to organize tools and other goodies in your garage. You simply mount the board to the wall and insert pegs to hang your tools and other frequently used items.

In this project, we started with a cluttered corner and turned it into an organized space by investing less than $100 and an afternoon worth of time.

Above: *This grim little corner of the garage is in bad need of attention. Not only is the space being used inefficiently, it's an eyesore. For starters, measure your available space carefully. You'll need to find the studs so you know where you can nail on the supports. Find a stud and then figure out how much area you can cover. I recommend that both edges of the pegboard hang on a stud. Bear in mind that most studs are separated by 16 inches (center to center), so you should plan the width of your pegboard accordingly.*

Right: *Once you have a plan in place and your supplies in hand, you can mount the first support to the stud. Predrill the supports to prevent them from splitting, and fasten the pegboard to the wall with a 2 1/2–inch wood screw.*

Make sure the support is level, then drill and screw the rest of it to the wall.

Edge the area you are planning to cover with pegboard. Note the middle support piece running horizontally to give you additional strength for hanging heavier items. Also, a 4-inch-wide pine board on the right gives plenty of backing to attach the pegboard where the two sheets butt together.

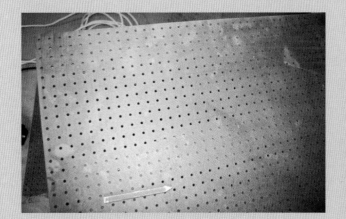

Above: Cutouts for outlets require you to measure from the top and the bottom of the pine edging. Double-check your measurements and that you have your hole on the correct edge, then cut the hole out with a jigsaw.

Right: To square up the corners, cut right to the line, back up, and round out the corner. You'll have to come back from the other direction to square up the corner.

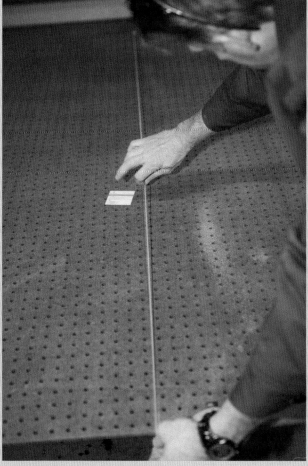

Above left: *In order to cut the sheet down to size, mark the edge carefully. If you trust your coordination, mark the cut by using a tape measure as shown, sliding it along the edge with a pencil in your hand. This works better for short spans.*

Above right: *You can also mark cuts with a chalk line. Carefully mark each end of the border, tighten the string, and snap it with your fingers to leave a blue line of chalk.*

Left: *Once the sheet is cut to fit, lift it up and mount it in place. Carefully line it up on your pine backing boards and screw it in place.*

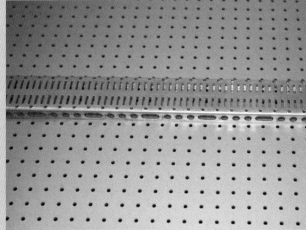

Left: *You can use 1 1/2-inch screws to hold the pegboard sheets on the backing. The no. 8 washers widen the screw's footprint and make for a sturdier mount.*

Above: *This tool bar was mounted on top of the project to hang garden rakes, shovels, and canoe paddles. The bar provides additional strength, as it is fastened to the pegboard with eight 2 1/2-inch wood screws..*

Below: *The finished project is better organized, better-looking, and costs less than $100.*

Above: *Sturdy metal shelves can be purchased at home improvement stores and work well for storing heavier parts and tools.*

Right: *This cleanly finished garage uses a huge set of cabinets to provide storage space, along with a slick little shoe caddy by the house entrance.*
Husnik Homes

continued from page 109

Shelving

Where does all that extra crap you have go? On shelves, of course. You have lots of options here, ranging from expensive gaudiness to home-built specials. Mr. Cheapskate, here's another chance for you to practice *wabi-sabi* and build some shelves.

Standalone shelving units are the simplest to build and the sturdiest, to boot. Construction doesn't get much simpler. A basic unit can be built by nailing together 1/2-inch plywood sheets. If you want to get fancy (and have a router or a table saw), cut 1/4-inch grooves for the shelves and use wood glue and screws to hold the unit together. You can also nail narrow strips of plywood below each shelf mounting point to provide additional support.

Left: If you have a little space, a set of shelves set in rows can be used to store all kinds of things.

My personal favorite is to build the legs and supports out of 2x4s and make the shelves out of 1/2-inch plywood. I like a bottom shelf that is about 18 inches tall for big stuff, and the top shelves spaced out at 12 inches. If you build a 64-inch-high unit, this will give you a five-shelf unit.

Be sure to drive your nails in at a downward angle, which will make the shelves better able to hold heavy loads. Nail it to your wall, and you'll add some strength and stability.

If you want a shelf unit with adjustable shelves, you'll have to use pins or another system to allow that flexibility. You can find plans online. If you have the time and inclination, they are a nice option.

You can improve the flexibility of the units by mounting them on casters, allowing you to easily move them around your garage even when they are full of your junk.

You can also buy standalone shelving units at your local home improvement retailer. The heavy-duty plastic units cost between $20 and $80 and are reasonably sturdy and easy to assemble.

Wooden shelving units are also available, and even retailers like Target and IKEA have cheap units for sale.

Right: *Another example of how cabinets can be used to mix storage space and workspace.*

These cost a bit more than building your own and are typically not as sturdy.

 If you have access to warehouse auctions, you can purchase used industrial units for very reasonable prices. I have a friend who gets me into these events, and I bought some nice 8-foot-long and 6-foot-high wire shelving units for about $20 each. These are great for storing camping supplies, paint, old computer equipment, and other things that don't see a lot of regular use.

The sturdiest units are designed to hold engines, transmissions, and other very heavy items. These are typically constructed with heavy steel beams topped by thick particle board and reinforced with steel crossbeams. If you can find an engine or industrial supply house that is going out of business, you can pick these up fairly reasonably.

If you want to store things higher up in your garage, line the top 4 feet or so of your garage with wall-mounted shelves. You can buy sturdy L-shaped brackets at your home building retail store and top them with two or three 6-inch-wide 3/4-inch boards. This type of storage allows you to reserve your floor space for lawn mowers, motorcycles, snowblowers, and other mobile items.

You can spend a lot of money on shelves, particularly if you want shelving units that match your cabinets and workbench. If your garage is a show place, Moneybags, go to it. Your neighbors will be jealous, and your place will look great.

Cabinets

If you want to store all your junk out of sight and behind closed doors, cabinets are the ticket. Going cheap requires a bit of effort, but, never fear, it can be done.

Building simple cabinets is one option. You can find plans online, of course (Plans Now has some elaborate and attractive cabinet systems you can build at home), but building your own cabinets is time consuming. And unless you are pretty handy with woodworking, they are going to look crude.

Again, Moneybags, you have it easy. Pick out one of the great-looking cabinet systems available and write a big check. Your garage will look great. We're all happy for you.

What's a cheapskate to do? Well, you can look into plastic cabinet systems. You can find these at large home improvement retailers. Companies like Rubbermaid make cabinets of all shapes and sizes, ranging in prices from $50 to $200 per cabinet.

You can also order a cabinet system and assemble and install it yourself. Costs are comparable to plastic units, but the finished product is nicer looking and a bit sturdier. But neither of these options is truly cheap.

 True cheapskates can try re-use centers. You can find old cabinets here for next to nothing, and a good center will likely have something to fit your space. Again, if you can get into industrial supply auctions where old equipment from factories is sold, you can find some deals.

Install Garage Cabinets

Supplies: Cabinet kit (purchased from manufacturer)
Tools: Cordless drill, 1/4-inch drill bit, Chuck and Phillips bit, Phillips screwdriver, pencil , level, measuring tape
Time: 1 hour
Tab: $80+

Cabinet installation is something that the garage owner can do. On a large installation, this can save hundreds of dollars. Bear in mind, however, that installation is not quite as simple as you might think. *Assembling* the cabinets, on the other hand, is relatively simple, particularly with the Slide-Lok cabinets used for this project.

The tricky part is squaring the cabinets up with the wall. Even in new garages, walls are rarely straight, and you will have to shim the cabinets in order to make everything line up flush. When you install only one or two cabinets, this is not terribly difficult, but expect to put some serious time in if you install a whole wall full of cabinets.

Assemble the cabinets and test fit everything before you start screwing things to the wall. This will allow you to figure out where you need shims and carefully put together a set of cabinets that are flush and square. And if you want a large bank of cabinets to be perfectly aligned, expect to spend a lot of hours shimming and fitting.

Slide-Lok cabinets assemble quickly and easily and come with detailed directions that show the process step by step. The panels for the cabinet are dovetailed and slide together quickly and simply. Run a 1/16-inch bead of glue in the joint and slide the end panels into the lower panel.

The cabinets are assembled as shown, with one side and two nailers glued and slid into place. The last panel slides down to complete the cabinet. Note that larger cabinets like this one are much easier to assemble if you have a second person helping out.

Little corner supports are screwed into the assembled cabinet to hold it together during installation. Slide-Lok cabinets will be a bit unstable until you screw them to the wall, as the design relies on the pressure of the nailer to provide rigidity. After screwing in the corner supports, plastic feet are fastened to the bottom of the cabinet, and the cabinet needs to sit at least 20 minutes to allow the glue to dry. Don't mount the cabinets until the glue is dry—gaps will open up in the front of the cabinet if you do.

Once the glue is dry, stand the cabinet in place. Carefully check to see how it lines up with the wall. This is the perfect time to put all the cabinets in place and determine where you need to place shims to align the cabinets.

Screw the cabinet to the wall through the nailer. Make sure to mark the location of your studs in the wall behind the cabinet.

The doors attach next. A standard screwdriver is more effective than a cordless drill to drive these screws, as you don't want to tighten them completely until the door is aligned.

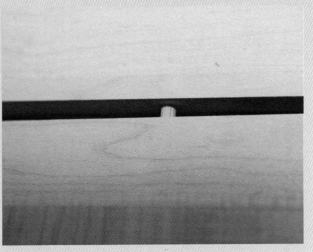

Left: *Assemble all the cabinets as shown and then do a test fit. See how these two cabinets fit tightly? That seam between the two would be open if they weren't square. Most walls will require you to put shims between the nailer and the wall for a tight fit. Expect to have to shim even if your garage is brand new.*

Above: *The cabinets fit together using dowels that line up the front of the cabinets.*

Once the cabinets are all in place and lined up, adjust the doors so that they close tightly and swing freely.

This good-looking cabinet set was put together in about an hour and cost less than $200.

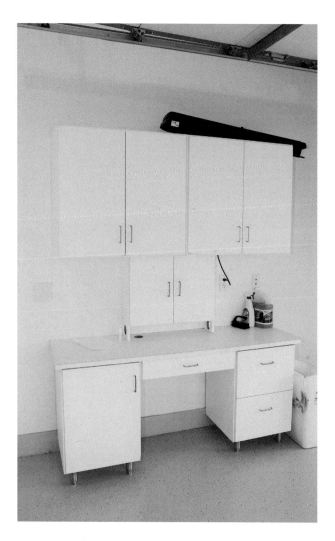

Above: *This cabinet installation combines a desk and storage space.*

Opposite: *A large rolling tool chest is the best and most common way to store your handtools. When starting out, purchase just the top piece of a rolling set.*

You can also try cabinet shops. They often have either old cabinets they ripped out of a house or something that was installed and then pulled out. This stuff is economical and serviceable.

OVERHEAD STORAGE

Garage ceilings are typically high, and that space can be a great place to store things, either on shelves suspended from the ceiling or by hanging things like canoes and bicycles from the ceiling.

The hanging platform (or loft) is my dad's favorite trick. He would simply build a solid platform to fit the space available—typically it was about 4x8 feet—and hang it securely from the rafters by sturdy chain or 2x4s.

You can find metal hanging platforms for sale for $50 to $100. These mount to your ceiling joists and typically are rated to hold several hundred pounds.

You can also build a garage loft by anchoring the platform to the wall on two sides and building a support beam to the floor on the outside corner. These are great for storing heavier items. You can access the loft with a home-built ladder that is permanently fixed, or simply use a stepladder.

Canoes and kayaks can be suspended from the ceiling by screwing a couple of heavy-duty ring bolts into the studs and using rope to pull the boat up. You can hang bicycles upside down with open hooks—simply space out the hooks so that the wheels slide in and the bike hangs up in the garage.

THE GARAGE FRIDGE

One of my favorite garage storage spaces is an old refrigerator I keep full of beer, water, and soda. You can buy dedicated garage fridges that come in all kinds of cool designs. Some are simply coated in galvanized metal to look cool, while others are designed to look like a toolbox or to match your entire garage cabinet system.

Cheapskates, listen up. If the fridge in your house is failing, buy a new one and put your old one in the garage. Or just put the word out to your friends. Often, you can find someone who is giving away a perfectly good fridge. Slide it in the garage and cover it with stickers so it fits the décor.

I did just that and made it a policy that anyone who came over had to bring a cool sticker for the fridge if they wanted a beer. It's now coated with motorcycle, hot rod, and other stickers.

ATTIC SPACE

The space above the joists in your garage is another great place to store things. If you have an open stud garage, you can simply slide things up there. This is great for lumber, skis, and other long, unwieldy items.

If your garage is sheetrocked, you'll want an access panel to the top of the garage.

When you build a new garage, consider adding a second floor. Even if you simply use a more steeply pitched roof, you'll economically create useful space.

The second floor is a great place to store all kinds of things. You can fill it with shelving units and put all your camping equipment up there, store old hot rod parts, or create a little corner where all of your fly-fishing gear is stored.

Access to the second floor is the key here, and this is another place where you can learn from my mistake. My

contractor clued me in to the fact that a second floor is a cheap way to add space, and I have a nice one with about 400 square feet and a 7-foot ceiling. And I installed the floor myself cheaply and relatively easily.

My mistake was the stairs. I put in one of the $75 folding units. You pull it down, unfold it, and climb up to the attic.

First, it's steep and awkward to haul big stuff up the ladder. I store my coolers up there, and the big one is a pain to drag up those narrow steps. I keep waiting for the day when I trip and fall off the ladder.

Also, when upstairs, you have a big hole in the floor to deal with. My neighbor built a knee wall around it for me, which made it safer, but you can still back up and step right into the hole if you aren't careful.

Lastly, the mechanism wore out after three years of use and had to be replaced with another one. These folding staircases are not made for regular use and will wear out quickly.

And then there is the heat loss. I heat my garage, and the door that closes when the stairs are raised is now three years old and doesn't seal very well. I need to put a cap over the hole to keep heat from escaping into the uninsulated second floor.

Still, pull-down stairs are an economical option to consider. If you don't go up to your second floor very often, they work.

 A better option is a full-on staircase. You have to dedicate some space on the ground floor if you put it inside the garage, but access to your second floor will be much better. You can also build the staircase on the outside of the garage and put an exterior door on the second floor.

The garage refrigerator is an essential addition. You can usually find one for next to nothing if you ask your friends and neighbors—people always seem to be upgrading to a new fridge in their house and looking to get rid of the old one.

Install an Overhead Storage Unit

Supplies: Overhead storage rack kit (purchased from manufacturer)

Tools: Rubber mallet, ladder, cordless drill, Chuck and Phillips bit, 3/16-inch drill bit, stud finder, 7/16-inch wrench, 7/16-inch socket and ratchet, pencil, level, measuring tape

Time: 30 minutes

Tab: $150–$250

In a garage, the least-utilized space is often high on the walls. A simple way to use that space is to install overhead storage racks. You can find a wide variety of these down at your local home improvement store, and many of the cheaper varieties work fine. If you want to put heavy things on your shelving, it's worth investing in some of the better models out there. One of the best is made by Onrax. These heavy-duty units use 1 3/4–inch lag bolts to fasten to the ceiling and are rated to hold up to 500 pounds. They are available in sizes that range from 2x4 feet to 8x4 feet.

Top: *The Onrax storage units used in this project hang from angle brackets that are bolted into studs with 1 3/4-inch lags. Use a stud finder to locate the stud in your ceiling, mark the holes on the ceiling to drill, and then drill 3/16-inch pilot holes for the lag bolts.*

Middle: *Bolt the first angle bracket to the ceiling with a lag bolt and a washer. Don't tighten it up all the way—leave a little free play so the bracket can move a bit as you install the unit.*

Bottom: *You can measure from your first bracket to determine where to mount the second bracket to the ceiling. We chose to double-check the location by attaching the upright angle posts to the crossbeams, bolting the top of the upright angle posts to the angle bracket on the ceiling, and making sure everything fit perfectly. The bolts that hold the upright angle posts to the angle brackets use washers on both sides.*

From the bolted-in angle brackets, measure out from the wall the width of the rack (24 inches, in this case).

Mark the drill holes carefully.

Drill two 3/16-inch pilot holes for the lag bolts and bolt the angle bracket in place with a lag bolt and washer.

Once you have all four angle brackets in place, assemble the upright angle posts onto the long crossbeams, and fasten them to the angle brackets in the ceiling.

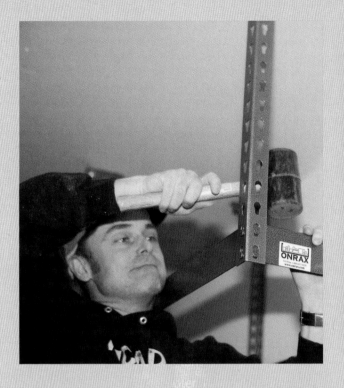

The side beams slide in next. The beams may need a light tap with a rubber mallet to seat completely.

Place the wire deck on the bolted-together rack.

Left: *Go back and tighten all the bolts.*

Above: *Now you have a 500-pound-capacity storage space in your garage.*

CHAPTER 6
GEARHEAD TOOLS

Tools are a garage owner's best friend. With the right ones, you can build, fix, or restore pretty much anything. Ask Jeff Spicoli or Tim Allen—tools rule.

You can go crazy and stock your garage with every tool known to exist, and you will be set no matter what happens. If you have the dough and the inclination, knock yourself out. Order the entire Snap-on catalog and fill gleaming cabinets full of impact swivel sockets, three-jaw slide-hammer pullers, and hydraulic nut splitters. Plus, you'll need to lace the garage with air lines and an exhaust-gas analyzer, and (naturally) install a 6-ton in-ground automotive lift.

What's that? You don't want to invest $1,720 in a hydraulic nut splitter, much less $10,000 in a lift? Well, read on. The truth is that you can invest a reasonable amount of money in the right tools and have most anything you need.

Good mechanics work with the tools they have. South American mechanics are legendary, particularly a group of guys who accompany Caravana, an annual motorcycle and ATV expedition that crosses the most remote parts of Bolivia. These guys have resurfaced valves with rubber hose and repaired holed engine cases with rolled bits of bamboo.

Bear that in mind next time you start to think you can't do a job because you are missing a tool. Be creative and you can get it done.

And since you aren't fixing machines in the middle of the Amazon jungle, if a job comes up that requires a tool you don't have, you now have an excuse to go down to the shop and pick it up. You get to buy a new tool, and because you are doing the work yourself, you'll probably save money even after you buy the tool (unless it happens to be a Snap-on hydraulic nut splitter).

If you don't have a good set of hand tools, go down to Sears to pick up a Craftsman set.

Yes, you can find cheaper tools or even hit the garage sales, classifieds, eBay, or Craigslist and buy a set of used tools. I applaud the effort if you do. The ideal situation is

A two-post lift is most often used in commercial applications and provides better access to your vehicle than the four-post variety. They also take up less space in the shop but are not as useful for storing vehicles. These are priced from $1,800 for low-end units to more than $4,000 for well-equipped commercial models.

Good hand tools are well worth the investment. Craftsman brand tools are reasonably priced and come with a lifetime warranty, making them a good choice for the hobbyist.

Basic Hand Tools for Mechanical Work

Socket ratchets, 1/4-, 3/8-, and 1/2-inch drives
Standard and deep-well socket sets (SAE and metric) for all three drives
Combination wrench sets (SAE and metric)
Screwdriver set (Phillips and standard bits)
Torx wrench set
Allen wrench set
Rubber mallet
Framing hammer
Sledge hammer
Impact wrench
Vise grips (small and large)
Pliers set
Wire stripper
File set

to find someone selling a complete set of mechanic's tools.

 Most mechanics own their tools, and you might come across a mechanic getting out of the business. These won't be cheap, but you'll probably have more tools than you'll ever need, and these are typically sold in high-quality rolling tool chests.

You can buy cheap tool sets at auto parts stores and big-box retailers. These tool sets generally are sold for less than $20 and are a rip-off at half that price. Sure, they're OK for someone who wants a tool set in the closet to tighten a bolt once every two years, but they are a waste of money for anyone who intends to actually use them. The ratchets break under any serious strain, the sockets snap and fit poorly, and the plastic-handled screwdriver sets shatter under pressure. Don't waste your money on this junk. You can find decent midlevel tools at your local hardware or home improvement store. Stanley screwdrivers, for example, are cheap and work fine.

As previously stated, when it comes time to buy hand tools, your best bet is to head down to Sears. You can buy a nice set of Craftsman hand tools for less than $600. Be sure it includes the pieces you'll need (see sidebar). You'll have a complete set of good-quality tools that come with a lifetime warranty (you won't be a real home mechanic until you break a Sears tool and take it in to get it replaced).

You'll notice that most professionals use Snap-on, SK, or another high-end brand. Pick up one of these tools, and you'll get an idea why—they generally feel better in your hand and are more sturdily built than the Sears tools. They are also significantly more expensive.

For example, a Snap-on 1/2-inch drive ratchet retails for $109, while the Craftsman unit goes for $20.99. That's a big price difference for a tool that you might use once a month.

The part of the price difference that you don't see is that brands like Snap-on and SK cater to professionals. They send a truck around to deliver tools on a regular basis, so if you are working at a dealership, for example, and you break a ratchet, you can get another one off the truck when they stop by. You can also get information from the rep about how to use certain tools and find out about new products offered by the company.

These services aren't available to home users, so high-end tools for home use are a luxury rather than a necessity.

TOOL CHESTS

The best way to store tools is in a large, rolling tool chest. They come with tons of handy little drawers to organize everything, and you can roll them next to your project so the tools are readily at hand.

How much of a tool chest you need depends, of course, on how many tools you have. If you are just starting out, a good way to go is just to purchase the top piece of a rolling set. The tool chests with drawers are the way

to go, as you can organize the tools and find the tool you need much more easily.

The top chest should have lots of small drawers, with two or three full-width drawers and two or three rows divided up into three drawers across. This allows you plenty of space to organize a full tool set.

Bottom chests are available as simple cabinets with a variety of drawers, or even just as a rolling cart with an open bottom. Look for one with casters so it rolls around the garage. If you are going to use it for hand-tool storage, look for one with several larger, full-width drawers for big tools at the bottom and a couple of narrow full-width drawers at the top.

You can find middle chests as well, particularly if you look at the higher-end brands. If you are a professional mechanic, you may have so many tools that you need

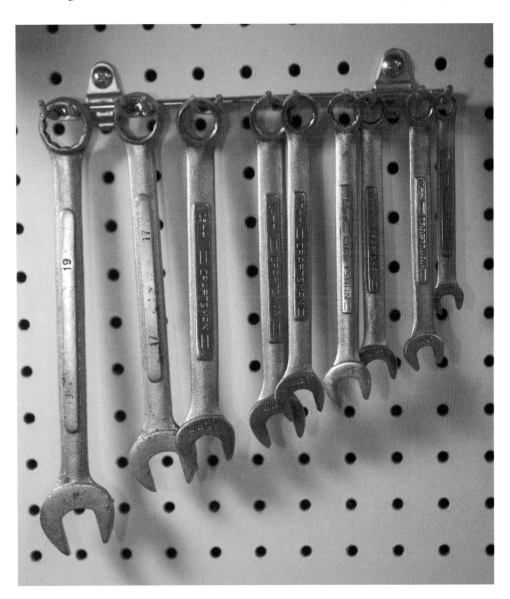

Commonly used tools can be hung on pegboard for easy access. Note that these hangers screw into the pegboard and cannot pull out when you take a tool off the peg.

A good rolling toolbox is another gearhead garage essential. The Craftsman units are decent, but there are a number of quality brands on the market that provide equal or better value.

three chests to hold them all. For most hobby mechanics, two chests are plenty.

As you get into a larger set of tools, a drawered cabinet is pretty much a necessity if you want to be able to find anything quickly. You can pick up a top-and-bottom set at Sears from just under $200 to about $500.

 The Craftsman boxes are serviceable and priced competitively but are not terribly well built. Stack-On, Waterloo, and Remline brand tool chests are nicer units, with heavier-duty components and drawers that roll out with more precision. They run between $400 and $2,200 for a top-and-bottom chest set, so the cost is significantly higher.

At the top of the food chain are brands like Kennedy, SK, and Snap-on. A top chest alone will cost about $500. These are designed to last for a lifetime of regular use and are ruggedly built units. If you can find these used, they can be a good deal, as they simply don't wear out.

CAR LIFTS

The ultimate gearhead garage accessory is a lift for your vehicle. This puts the vehicle up in the air so you can get underneath it (cars and trucks) or work on it while standing up (motorcycles).

At the most basic level, you can lift your car with a rolling hydraulic automotive jack. These come in a variety of capacities. If you plan to work under your car, purchase some jack stands to place under the car after you have it jacked up. Lower the car onto the jack stands before you crawl underneath it to help prevent it from moving and falling on top of you.

You can also equip your garage with an automotive lift that picks up the entire car. These are available as low-rise, two- and four-post, scissors, and in-ground lifts. The low-rise lift is designed for the home user and is a compact unit that lifts the vehicle about 24 inches off the ground. This is perfect for changing oil, rotating tires, or working on your brakes.

You will probably need a 220-volt power outlet for the unit, and you may have clearance issues with overhead garage doors that roll up into a track. In some cases, a solid lift-type door can solve this.

Four-post automotive lifts are more common for home use and give you the ability to lift the car above your head. This is the most comfortable setup for working on the bottom side of the car, and a great setup for restorations and other tasks in which you will be working on your car for extended periods of time. Be sure the unit has enough capacity to lift your vehicle. Prices for four-post lifts range from $2,000 to much more.

Four-post lifts can be used for adding storage space as well as for working on your vehicle. For storage purposes, the lift is used to raise one vehicle in the air while another is driven underneath. These are even available with casters on the bottom so you can move them around the garage. They can also be equipped with full-width bottoms and/or drip trays so you don't have to worry about a leaky main seal in the top car dripping all over the paint of the machine below.

You'll need at least a 10-foot ceiling to use a four-post lift with two average-sized cars. Revolution Lifts has a nice online calculator that allows you to input the height of your cars and figure out how much ceiling height you'll require to store them.

Two-post lifts are another option. These lift the car over your head, take up a bit less space, and cost slightly less than four-post lifts. Scissor-type lifts are a third option.

 In-ground lifts are the ultimate (and most expensive), as the mechanicals are all concealed under the floor. Obviously, these should be installed when you pour the concrete.

MOTORCYCLE AND ATV LIFTS

Working on a motorcycle while sitting on the floor requires a lot of bending over that gets tiresome quickly. The solution is a lift that raises the bike 24 to 36 inches. The cheapest units lift the vehicle manually and can be had for about $500. Others use air pressure or hydraulic jacks and run about $1,000. Cheapskates can simply build a low wooden table and use ramps to roll the bike on top.

Whichever you use, be sure to fasten the bike with tie-downs so it doesn't pop off the platform while you are working on it!

ATV enthusiasts can use the same platform lifts as above, or find small, rolling lifts for less than $100 that will raise the machine about 20 inches, which is plenty for changing tires, suspension, and so on.

COMPRESSORS AND AIR TOOLS

An air compressor is a great addition to a garage, useful for filling tires, blowing dirt out of old parts, and powering tools. If you just need to fill a tire here and there, buy the cheapest unit you can find and be done.

If you intend to power air tools, buy a compressor with an adequate rating of cubic feet per minute (CFM) and a tank large enough to accommodate your needs. You need at least 100 CFM for most air tools, so look for a compressor that pumps out 175 CFM or better (you want the rating to exceed the tool needs by a factor of 1.5 or better).

You also want to pay attention to the duty cycle, which refers to how long the compressor can run (i.e., supply air to your tools). A compressor with a 25 percent duty cycle can only run one-quarter of the time that it's on and pressurizing the tank. If you have it on for 60 minutes and during that time it supplies air to your tools for more than 15 minutes, the compressor could overheat. The highest-quality compressors have a 100 percent duty cycle, meaning they can run constantly and not overheat or fail.

Horsepower ratings of compressors really aren't all that important. Electric and gas-powered compressors use

---

Basic Tools for Building Wooden Stuff

For most of the projects in this book, you only need a few simple woodworking tools. Here's a list that will get you set up. All are tools that you will most likely have for the rest of your life. As such, I recommend you purchase quality equipment rather than the low-end stuff. You can find quality tools at any home improvement store, and they will last a long time.

Framing hammer
25-foot measuring tape
Square
24-inch (or longer) level
Cordless drill
Drill bit set
Screwdriver bits for drill
Hand saw
Circular saw
Chalk line
Screwdriver set (Phillips and standard bits)
Socket set (SAE sizes, 3/8- and 1/2-inch drives)
Open-end wrenches (SAE sizes)
Pry bar
Vise grip set
Pliers set
Wood file
Sawhorses

different types of horsepower ratings for starters. In the end, it's the CFM that matters—not horsepower.

WELDERS

For restorers, hot rodders, and fabricators, a welder is an essential tool that allows you to join metal objects together. A MIG (metal inert gas) welder is the place to start, as they are the easiest to use. You'll need to keep a fire extinguisher nearby, as most beginning welders seem to develop a knack for starting things on fire. Come to think of it, you should have at least one fire extinguisher in your garage whether or not you own a welder.

If you decide to add welding to your garage repertoire, be sure to allow for adequate space and power. You'll want a metal welding bench and a 220-volt power supply. Expect to spend at least $500 for a good welder, and be prepared to buy a mask and gloves as well.

I strongly recommend you do some reading before jumping in. Try the excellent *Welding Basics* or the *Welder's Handbook* by Richard Finch.

Above: *A welder is an essential tool for the home fabricator. A MIG wire-feed welder is the best place to start for beginners, as it gives you the best results with relatively little experience.*

Left: *If you plan to store engines, a wheeled cart makes moving your big-block Ford V-8 a bit easier.*

Opposite: *The four-post automotive lift is great for storage and for working on vehicles. Revolution Lifts builds this four-post model. Expect to pay between $1,500 and $2,500 for a good four-post lift.* Revolution Lifts

PARTS WASHERS

Another great gearhead tool is a parts washer. These are sinks that come in a variety of sizes and have pump systems integrated so you can squirt chemical cleaner on parts. Some mount on the wall, while others are on legs. The least expensive units are designed to sit on bench tops.

You can find cheapo units down at your local parts store for less than $100, while industrial units run $1,000 or more.

Cheapskates, outfitting one of those big stainless-steel sinks with a pump that squirts cleaning fluid will do the job.

Note that the fluids used in the parts washers range from ultratoxic to relatively environmentally friendly citrus-based fluids. The citrus stuff also smells better than the toxic stuff and, as an added bonus, won't peel off your skin.

Below: *Jack stands keep your car up in the air and are a necessary safety measure if you plan to work underneath your car.*

Above: *Mount your vise on the end of a bench so that you can easily clamp large or long objects in it.*

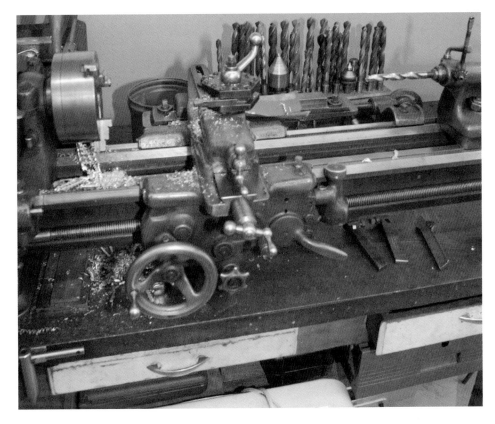

Left: *A lathe is a high-end garage tool that allows you to mill metal parts.*

Below: *A spray booth is perhaps the ultimate home garage accessory, a sealed space used for painting.*

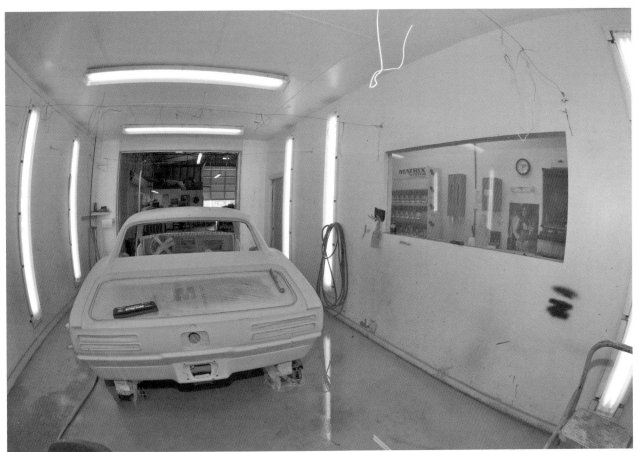

It Ain't Easy Being Green, II: Disposing of the Nasty Stuff

Garages generate all sorts of hazardous materials. Here are a few tips that can help you deal with them.

Drained Oil and Used Oil Filters

According to the American Petroleum Institute (API), more than 600 million gallons of motor oil are purchased each year, and it takes only 1 gallon of improperly disposed oil to contaminate a million gallons of groundwater. More than 40 percent of our nation's oil pollution comes from used motor oil dumped by people who change their own oil.

So if you care just a little bit about the world your grandkids will inherit, pour your old oil into some kind of sealable container and take it down to your local recycling center or service station (most will take it for free, typically on specific times and dates). Check with city hall or your local service station to find out who will take the old oil.

Bear in mind that 2 gallons of re-used oil provide enough potential energy to watch television for 7 1/2 days straight (an entire NASCAR season).

Buy your oil in gallon jugs, and you can dump the old oil right in to the used containers when you are done. Old milk or water jugs work well for this too. Don't use bleach, solvent, gasoline, or household cleaner containers for your drained oil.

You can also recycle oil filters at many service stations. Again, check with your local station on this one. If they won't take the filters, drain the old filter for 12 hours or so before throwing it out.

Antifreeze and Other Nasty Liquids

Antifreeze, fuel additives, carburetor cleaner, starting fluid, brake fluid, and transmission fluid are all extremely toxic to the environment. Pouring them down the drain can and will screw up your environment and get you in trouble with the EPA if you get busted.

Bottle it up and save it until you can get rid of it at your local recycling center. Check with www.earth911.com to locate a hazardous waste disposal center near you.

Batteries

Recycling batteries is not as simple as it might seem, mainly because there are lots of different kinds of batteries. If you *don't* recycle batteries, you'll be happy to know that you pollute lakes and streams with metals that vaporize when they are burned, add heavy metals to solid-waste landfills, and fill your environment with lead and acid.

The chart below is designed to help you determine what you can and can't recycle. Keep in mind that this chart isn't hard and fast. Check with your municipality: if they offer curbside recycling or a central recycling center, they may take your expired alkaline, Ni-Cd, and lithium batteries.

Car batteries need to go to special centers for recycling—you can't just stick them out on the curb with the rest of your recycling. Take the battery back to the place you bought the new one—most retail centers have an exchange program and will dispose of it for you.

Tires

The obvious thing to do is take your tires down to your local service station, and they'll get rid of them for you for a modest fee. You can also hang a rope off a tree and tie an old tire to the end of it for your kids to play on or make one of 50 home projects done with old tires found in the book *Tire Recycling Is Fun* published by Paul Farber (see appendix for contact information)

Battery	Common Name	Use	Sizes Available	How to Dispose
Alkaline, Manganese	Coppertop, Alkaline	Flashlights, remote controls, transistor radios	AAA, AA, C, D, 6V, 9V	Place in the trash.
Button	Mercuric oxide, silver oxide, lithium, alkaline, Zinc-air	Watches, hearing aids, remote controls	Varies	Take to a household hazards collection site; use the locator tool at www.earth911.com.
Carbon Zinc	Heavy duty, general purpose	Flashlights, remote controls, transistor radios	AAA, AA, C, D, 6V, 9V	Place in the trash.
Lead Acid Vehicle Batteries	DieHard, Yuasa, Exide, Optima, Autolite, Motorcraft, TrueStart, Duralast, EverStart	Cars, trucks, motorcycles	12V, many sizes and shapes	Send or take it to the place you bought the new one.
Lithium	"Lithium" label on the battery	Cameras, calculators	3V, 6V, 3V button	Requires special center; use the locator tool at www.rbrc.com to find one.
Nickel-Cadmium (rechargeable)	Labeled "Ni-Cad"	Cell phones, power tools	AAA, AA, C, D, 6V, 9V	Requires special center; use the locator tool at www.rbrc.com to find one.
Rechargeable Alkaline	Renewal	Flashlights, remote controls, transistor radios	AAA, AA, C, D	Place in the trash.
Sealed Lead Acid (rechargeable)	Gel, VRB, AGM, Cyclone, El Power, Dynasty, Gates, Lithonia, Saft, Panasonic, Yuasa	Power tools, kids' ATVs, metal detectors	2V, 6V, 12V	Requires special center; use the locator tool at www.rbrc.com to find one.

Information for this chart courtesy of Environmental Health & Safety Online (www.ehso.com)

Left upper: *Oil filters are also recyclable and some states ban them from being thrown into landfills. You can find out where to recycle filters at www.filtercouncil.com.*

Left lower: *Used oil should be saved in plastic containers and recycled. You can make do with milk jugs or other screw-top plastic containers. Note that you shouldn't store used motor oil in containers that originally housed chemicals.*

Below: *Oil spills can be cleaned up using an absorbent granular material like Floor-Dry or kitty litter. The spill should be covered up overnight. Then sweep up the mess and throw it into the garbage can.*

CHAPTER 7
MAKING THE MOST OF GARAGE SPACE

When Joe decided to build a garage next to his home in West St. Paul, Minnesota, he wanted to add as much space as humanly possible without violating the city's building codes.

He wanted some office space for his home-contracting business, a couple of bathrooms, and a room for his kids to play in. His solution was to cleverly tuck in the trusses and add two dormers to his 24x40 garage. The result of his clever design gave him about 700 square feet of heated finished space above his garage.

He not only does his office work up there while his kids play across the hall, he also uses the space to host parties and family gatherings. Joe isn't alone in his creative use of garage space. In garages across the country, you'll find people who customize their spaces to play and record music, play video games, build climbing walls, or get groups together to race slot cars, among countless other pursuits.

One of the easiest ways to make your garage a good place to hang out is to add a garage door screen. This covers your garage door opening to keep bugs out and essentially gives you a two-car screened porch.

On the simplest level, you can also add an entryway, mudroom, or laundry room. These are particularly useful in an attached garage, as you buy space in the house.

Creating an in-garage office, game room, or hobby room is a good way to take advantage of the extra space to be found in your garage. You can simply set off the back half of the space with a dividing wall or, again, take advantage of the second floor.

Like Joe, you can add a second floor to your garage fairly economically (see Chapter One), and it's a great way to add usable space to the structure. Add dormers, and you'll find half a house worth of space that can be made into a den, hobby room, office, or play room.

Bear in mind that home offices are an increasingly smart addition as more and more Americans telecommute. Between 2004 and 2006, the number of people

Your garage space doesn't have to be dedicated entirely to your vehicles. Garages house everything from climbing walls and art studios to slot car tracks and places to hang out with your friends—all with your over-the-top car collection in full view.

working at home increased 65 percent, according to a study by The Dieringer Research Group.

In larger garages, a loft is a great way to create some space to entertain and overlook your collection of Corvette race cars, Triumph Triples, or Scott Flying Squirrel motorcycles.

Kitchens are also nice additions if you intend to entertain in your garage. And even if you don't want to deal with plumbing a full kitchen, a bar and a refrigerator go a long way toward making your garage more hangout friendly.

Gearhead sorts often create spaces to store models, memorabilia, and other goodies they collect that are related to their passion. Some of my favorite garages do this without much planning at all—the owners just cover the walls with goodies that they come across.

If you have a lot of space, a projection screen that hits a big blank white wall and some old couches and chairs can make a great little home theater.

The garage is also a great place to put a hot tub. If you want to go all out, enclose the tub in a cedar-paneled room and add a changing room. Just be sure to allow for adequate ventilation to abate the moisture.

If you have a non-gearhead type spouse or housemate, consider adding a room that caters to his or her hobby. You can easily add a woodworking shop, sculpture studio, or even a rock-climbing wall to your garage.

Entertaining in the garage is a natural. It's away from your house and it provides a great open space for hosting large groups. If you don't have the cash for a stainless steel–coated bar and sink, simply put some bean dip and a tub of beer on the workbench.

Above: The garage provides a lot of square footage that can be used for much more than vehicle-related pursuits. This loft is outfitted with a kitchen and giant slot car track for entertaining.

Left: A pool table and living area opposite from a slot car track and kitchen make this garage the ultimate car-nut hangout.

Opposite top: Kitchen and break room areas are nice additions to a garage. Note how this one uses aluminum spars to form a faux ceiling.

Opposite bottom: The garage hangout is the perfect place to put furniture that doesn't have a place in your home. It's the garage—the most important thing is comfort. And where else are you going to put a display case full of vintage Matchbox toys? Merchants who are shuttering their doors are a good source for display cases.

Above: *A blank wall and a projection television can turn your garage into a movie and entertainment center.*

Opposite: *You can use the garage as a display area for your latest memorabilia acquisitions, not to mention your Allard race car.*

Left: *A logical addition to a garage is a home office. It doesn't have to be this over the top—a simple office adds value to the home as more and more people begin telecommuting to work.*

A home office can be added to a garage fairly simply. This one was built for less than $4,000 and features in-floor heat, air conditioning, and cable and power hookups. The office serves as a daily workspace and is a great place to play poker and drink beer.

Here, part of a shop has been converted into a home. One of the interesting touches is the incorporation of the tin roof into the ceiling of the living room.

The guys from The Texican Chop Shop hang out after a long day of building street rods. The garage is a great place to do just that, whether it's a palace or an old one-car that houses your '73 Pinto.

This finished space was built by Jack Dant as a place to paint and hang out. Some of the unique features include the flooring, which is finished plywood, and corrected lighting appropriate for painting. Dant installed the shelving built in to the knee wall visible at left as well. The project took more than three years to complete, but the result is ideally suited to the owncr's needs.

If you can't afford vintage race cars, you can coat your toolbox with cool stickers. Or just cut out your own ratted-out Superman logo, as the guys at the Texican Chop Shop did. The Texican Chop Shop is owned by the band Los Lonely Boys, who put their mark in the new concrete poured for the building.

Neon signs, posters, and even old bumper cars can serve as decoration for your wrench palace.

Above: *This shop is completely over the top, containing everything from vintage light bulbs to period* Playboy *magazines. It also is probably the most complete collection of Veltex petroliana in existence.*

Left: *To hell with white elephants—decorate with junked cylinder heads.*

Opposite: *Neon is always a winner in the garage.*

Above: *If you can find an old* Miss Budweiser *lying around, lean her up against the wall. Who needs posters?*

Opposite: *Vintage race bikes also make great decoration.*

Following pages: *Obscene quantities of chrome are sure winners for the garage owner.*

MAKING THE MOST OF GARAGE SPACE

RESOURCES

Garage Floor Heating

Orbit Radiant Heating
1507 Park Ave.
Perkasie, PA 18944
888-895-0958 or 215-453-9228
Sales@OrbitMfg.com
www.OrbitMfg.com
Suppliers of radiant heating.

Infloor Radiant Floor Heating Systems
920 Hamel Rd.
Hamel, MN 55340
800-608-0562
info@infloor.com
www.infloor.com
Suppliers of radiant heating.

Steibel Eltron
17 West St.
West Hatfield, MA 01088
info@stiebel-eltron-usa.com
413-247-3380
800-582-8423
www.stiebel-eltron-usa.com
Manufacturer of tankless water heaters and
other energy-efficient heating and electrical
products.

Microtherm Inc.
223 Airtex
Houston, TX 77090
1-888-296-9293
deseitz@attglobal.net
Manufactures Seisco tankless water heaters.
Some Seisco units are sold under the brand
name "Hydro Shark."

Consumer Information

Rip-off reports
www.ripoffreport.com
To file complaints about companies or
individuals.

Energy Star
1200 Pennsylvania Ave. NW
Washington, DC 20460
888-782-7937
www.energystar.gov
Department of Energy ratings that relate to
energy use and energy efficiency in homes
designed by builders.

Recycling

Recycling Research Institute
PO Box 4430
Leesburg, VA 20177
571-258-0500
sales@scraptirenews.com
www.scraptirenews.com
Publication devoted to providing news and
information about tire and rubber recycling.

Earth 911
Global Alerts, LLC
14646 N. Kierland Blvd.
Scottsdale, AZ 85254
480-889-2650
trey.granger@globalalerts.com
www.earth911.com
Recycling information and locator.

Rechargeable Battery Recycling Corporation
(RBRC)
1000 Parkwood Cir., Ste. 450
Atlanta, GA 30339
678-419-9990
recycling@rbrc.com
www.rbrc.org
Organization that recycles cell phone and
other batteries. Web site lists drop-off points
around the United States.

General Retailers

The Garage Store, LLC
2705 Lake Crest Dr.
Flower Mound, TX 75022
800-441-1552
Sales@MyGarageStore.com
www.mygaragestore.com
Catalogs and online retail outlets.

America's Pride
75 County St.
Seekonk, MA 02771
800-348-4244
508-336-9629
websales@americasprideonline.com
www.americasprideonline.com
Retailer of cabinets, shelving, and other
storage units.

Garage Boyz
Calgary, AB
Victoria, BC
866-711-2699
403 701-2699
info@garageboyz.ca
http://www.garageboyz.ca
Garage Boyz has a cool calculator that lets
you put together your entire garage,
including a from-ground-up blueprint to
build and outfit the garage.

Elite Xpressions LLC
4833 Saratoga Blvd. PMB 138
Corpus Christ, TX 78414
866-556-6324
361-906-0863
customerservice@elite-xpressions.com
www.elite xpressions.com
DIY high-quality garage storage systems.

Car Guy Garage, Inc.
4740 N. Cumberland Ave., Ste. 150
Chicago, IL 60656
800-736-9308
sales@carguygarage.com
www.carguygarage.com
Retailers of cabinets, workbenches, flooring,
and storage for the garage.

Global Industrial
Global Equipment Company, Inc.
2505 Mill Center Pkwy., Ste. 100
Buford, GA 30518
888-978-7759
sales@globalindustrial.com
www.globalindustrial.com
Retailers of industrial supplies, storage
equipment, and shelving.

Gladiator GarageWorks
553 Benson Rd., MD 8010
Benton Harbor, MI 49022
866-342-4089
www.gladiatorgw.com
Gladiator is a Whirlpool brand of garage
storage cabinets and more. Web site has
built-in planner to help lay out your floor
plan and estimate costs to outfit the garage
with Gladiator goodies.

Overhead Storage

ONRAX Overhead Storage Racks
30200 SE 79th St., Suite 120
Issaquah, WA 98027
866-637-8828
brad@onrax.com
www.onrax.com
Garage storage needs.

OverAll Storage
11891 Galena Ave.
Fountain Valley, CA 92708
714-964-6048
sales@overallstorage.com
www.overallstorage.com
Retailer of overhead storage solutions.

Stacks and Stacks
The Homewares Place
1045 Hensley St.
Richmond, CA 94801
800-761-5222
www.stacksandstacks.com
Items to design and organize your garage.

Benches and Small-Parts Drawers

LaBonia Company
Craftline Storage Products
PO Box 398
70 Stoddard Ave.
North Haven, CT 06473
800-505-9099
203-239-5681
sales@craftline.us
www.craftline.us
Quality modular storage products and
toolboxes.

PremierGarage Systems, LLC.
1616 West Williams Dr.
Phoenix, AZ 85027
888-664-9248
602-904-5805
http://premiergarage268-px.rtrk.com
The largest franchisor specializing in garage
improvements using state-of-the-art
technologies and materials.

JNK Products, LLC
1111 S. 7th St.
Grand Junction, CO 81501
877-873-3736
970-245-1416
support@jnkproducts.com
www.jnkproducts.com
Expansive selection of garage flooring and
garage floor products.

GarageCabinetsOnline.com
1309 Ponderosa Dr., Ste. 204B
Sandpoint, ID 83864
800-540-1695
sales@garagecabinetsonline.com
www.garagecabinetsonline.com
Garage storage cabinets and other storage
systems from America's top manufacturers.

The Organization Station
3825 E. Mainsail Blvd.
Tucson, AZ 85739
520-825-3015
sales@organizationstation.com
www.organization-station.com
Creates custom designs and layouts for
storage to suit your individual needs.

SLIDE-LOK Garage Interiors & Storage
Cabinets
437 W. Fairmont Dr.
Tempe, AZ 85282
800-835-1759
480-222-9720
customerservice@slide-lok.com
www.slide-lok.com
Modular garage cabinets and garage-floor
coatings.

TidyGarage Inc.
501 N. Elizabeth St.
Dearborn, MI 48128
888-4GARAGE
313-792-0629
www.tidygarage.com
Storage systems that allow you to transform
previously unused wall and ceiling space
into useful and productive storage.

Gupta Permold Corp.
Consumer Goods Division, DiamondLife
Brand
234 Lott Rd.
Pittsburgh, PA 15235
888-98-DGEAR x103
help@diamondlifegear.com
www.diamondlifegear.com
Cool diamond-plated pegboard, hanging
pegs, bins, and more for garage
organization.

Garage Refrigerator

MicroFridge Corporate Headquarters
10 Walpole Park S.
Walpole, MA 02081
800-994-0165
508-660-9200
www.microfridge.com
Product line includes combination units,
refrigerators, microwave ovens, and
electronic safes.

Floor Coatings

Citadel Floor Finishing Systems
3001 103rd Ln. NE
Blaine, MN 55449
866-765-4310
patrick@citadelfloors.com
www.citadelfloors.com
Manufacturer of polyaspartic polyurea
floor-coating systems.

Original Color Chips
26200 Groesbeck Hwy.
Warren, MI 48089
586-771-6500
800-227-8479
salesteam_occ@originalcolorchips.com
www.originalcolorchips.com
Custom floor-coating system and floor
finish, including glow-in-the-dark and
black-light-sensitive chips.

GarageFloor.com
JNK Products, LLC
1111 S. 7th St.
Grand Junction, CO 81501
888-8-Garage
sale@garagefloor.com
www.garagefloor.com
Garage floor sales and service.

Armorpoxy
939 Lehigh Ave.
Union, NJ 07083
888-755-7361
908-810-9613
info@armorpoxy.com
www.armorpoxy.com
Supplier of commercial-grade epoxy and
PVC tile, rubber mats, and garage-
organization bits, including slatwall.

SwissTrax, Inc.
82579 Fleming Way, Unit A
Indio, CA 92201
866-748-7940
760-347-3330
sales@swisstrax.com
www.swisstrax.com
Practical and modern alternative to standard
concrete and epoxy garage flooring.

Floorguard, Inc.
340 Marshall Ave., Unit 101
Aurora, IL 60506
888-694-2724
630-896-7040
customerservice@floorguard.com
www.floorguard.com
Maintenance-free garage systems with the
superior technology and materials.

Better Life Technology, LLC
9812 Pflumm Rd.
Lenexa, KS 66215
913-894-0403 ext. 21
customerservice@bltllc.com
www.bltllc.com
Produces garage-floor protector mats and
rollout garage-floor coverings.

RevTek
Rhino Sports of Boston
PO 208
Hopkinton, MA 01748
800-585-0922
774-277-1413
www.revtekgaragefloors.com
Sells interlocking mat tiles that require no
adhesives or special tools to install.

RaceDeck
Snap Lock Industries
2330 W. California Ave.
Salt Lake City, UT 84104
800-457-0174
www.racedeck.com
DIY garage-flooring systems made from high-impact copolymer that require no glues and produce no toxic fumes.

UCoat It
32106 Woodward
Royal Oak, MI 48073
800-UCoat-It
248-545-4055
www.ucoatit.com
Commercial-grade epoxy floor coatings in several colors and decorative options to suit virtually any décor.

Durall Concrete Floor Coatings
7723 Pillsbury Ave. S.
Minneapolis, MN 55423
800-466-8910
952-888-1488
info@concrete-floor-coatings.com
www.concrete-floor-coatings.com
Floor coating retailer.

Garage Kits
Shelter-Kit
22 W. Mill St.
Tilton, NH 03276
603-286-7611
buildings@shelter-kit.com
www.shelter-kit.com
Custom kit garages and homes.

Garage Design and Contracting
The American Institute of Architects (AIA)
1735 New York Ave. NW
Washington, DC 20006-5292
800-AIA-3837
202-626-7300
infocentral@aia.org
www.architectfinder.aia.org
Information about working with architects and references to reputable firms.

DiGiacomo Homes & Renovation, Inc.
11655 Ridgemount Ave. W.
Minnetonka, MN 55305
rgdigiacomo@earthlink.net
www.dghomesandrenovation.com
Architectural firm specializing in renewability.

James Barton Design Build, Inc.
5920 148th St. W., Ste. 100
Apple Valley, MN 55124
952-431-1670
Architectural firm.

Orfield Design & Construction, Inc.
4501 Minnetonka Blvd., 3rd Fl.
Saint Louis Park, MN 55416
952-920-6543
www.orfielddesign.com
Architectural firm.

Rehkamp Larson Architects, Inc.
2732 W. 43rd St.
Minneapolis, MN 55410
612-285-7275
info@rehkamplarson.com
www.rehkamplarson.com
Architectural firm.

Sussel Builders
54 Transfer Rd., Ste. 16B
St. Paul, MN 55114
651-645-0331
info@susselbuilders.com
www.susselbuilders.com
Builder and designer.

Plan3D, Inc.
8549 E. Tanque Verde
Tucson, AZ 85749
520-760-0852
support@plan3D.com
www.plan3d.com
Web-based home-design tool that lets you see ideas with dimensions in blueprint-like mode.

Garage Plan Sources
PlansNOW.com
August Home Publishing Company
2200 Grand Ave.
Des Moines, IA 50312
800-475-9259
515-875-7090
www.PlansNOW.com
Downloadable project plans and technique articles developed by the editors of *August Home Publishing*.

Work Bench Stuff
RDM Industrial Products, Inc.
1652 Watson Ct.
Milpitas, CA 95035
877-777-9130 or 408-945-8400
info@rdm-ind.com
www.rdm-ind.com
Computer monitor mounts and other accessories for your workbench.

The 5S Store
PO Box 834
Pepperell, MA 01463
978-842-4610
Sales@the5sstore.com
www.the5sstore.com
Pegboard accessories.

Lifts
Rotary Lift
2700 Lanier Dr.
Madison, IN 47250
800-640-5438
812-273-1622
userlink@rotarylift.com
Auto-lift products for use in the professional automotive service and commercial truck and transit markets.

Heavy Tools
KMS Tools and Equipment, Ltd.
110 Woolridge St.
Coquitlam, BC V3K 5V4
800-567-8979
604-522-5599
csr@kmstools.com
www.kmstools.com
Retailer of compressors, lathes, and welders.

Garage Doors and Accessories
autoCLOSER
Xceltronix
2813 Industrial Ln.
Garland, TX 75041
877-748-8366
972-690-5255.
sales@autocloser.com
www.autocloser.com
Retailer of an automatic garage door closing system and touch-keyed garage security system.

Garage Screens
Garage Door Screens
55648 Silver Creek Ln.
Macomb Twp, MI 48042
810-397-0301
customerservice@garagedoorscreens.com
www.GarageDoorScreens.com
Supplier of garage door screens that let the fresh air in and keep the bugs out.

Garage Forum
http://www.garagejournal.com/forum/
If you want to talk garage, this may be the best place on the Web to do so. Lots of good information about almost anything garage, as well as lots of people doing and posting interesting home garage projects.

INDEX

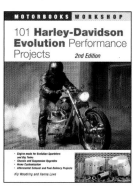

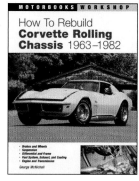
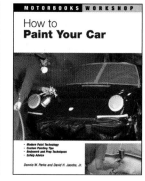